PRAY LIKE A CHAMPION TODAY

"In *Pray Like a Champion Today*, Fr. Nate Wills, CSC, captures something special—a unique exploration of the Notre Dame spirit. From the perspective of the sidelines, he connects the dots between football, family, and faith and illustrates the transformative power Our Lady's University has on students, alumni, and fans alike."

Dolly Duffy
Executive Director of the Notre Dame Alumni Association

"St. Paul himself, in the Bible, used sports as an analogy for the most sublime goal of all: reaching heaven. Fr. Nate is in good company as he colorfully and convincingly displays the deep spirituality of Notre Dame football, showing how there is a religious, transcendent side to this celebrated sport and to America's favorite football team. This is a touchdown!"

Cardinal Timothy M. Dolan
Archbishop of New York

PRAY LIKE A CHAMPION TODAY

Sacred Stories from the Sidelines of Notre Dame Football

FR. NATE WILLS, CSC
FIGHTING IRISH FOOTBALL CHAPLAIN

Founded in 1865, Ave Maria Press is a ministry of the United States Province of Holy Cross.

www.avemariapress.com

Paperback: ISBN-13 978-1-64680-425-2

E-book: ISBN-13 978-1-64680-426-9

Cover image © Notre Dame Athletics.

Cover and text design by Christopher D. Tobin.

Printed and bound in the United States of America.

Library of Congress Cataloging-in-Publication Data is available.

For my parents, Dan and Sue Wills—champions of love, support, and prayer for their children and grandchildren. Love you always.

CONTENTS

ND
FOOTBALL

FOREWORD

TEAM GLORY

As the head coach of the Notre Dame football program, I am often asked what our team goals will be for each season. My answer always remains the same: putting in the work necessary to reach our full potential and striving to achieve Team Glory.

Each year, the makeup of the program allows for a fluid answer on what our full potential may look like, but the idea of Team Glory remains steadfast.

What is Team Glory? That singular moment, celebrating TOGETHER, that feeling of pure joy achieved after a hard-fought victory.

I would go on to define Team Glory as putting the goals of the team ahead of any of your personal goals: sacrificing for the person to the left or right of you to achieve a common goal, and giving everything you have for Notre Dame, understanding that with Team Glory will come individual glory. Our goal each year is to reach our full potential, and as we strive to do that together, along the way we will attain Team Glory.

While we work relentlessly to achieve Team Glory, we must each perform our individual roles to our very best ability. Our team chaplain, Fr. Nate Wills, CSC, is someone we can trust to perform his role at his best ability each day. He leads the people in our program along their individual spiritual journeys, taking everyday moments and making connections to faith that are relatable and inspirational.

Just as Fr. Nate has mastered his role as our team chaplain, each person in our program is constantly striving to do the same in theirs. Whether it be the backup long snapper, the starting quarterback, the offensive coordinator, or a student manager, we are all on our own spiritual journeys—and, as our chaplain, Fr. Nate is there to serve us. He provides spiritual guidance, emotional support, and a nonjudgmental presence to team members, coaches, and staff, both on and off the field.

Not everyone in our program is Catholic, nor are they required to practice Catholicism, but Fr. Nate does a brilliant job of meeting people where they are in terms of faith. He has a natural ability to make people feel comfortable in sharing their authentic selves, and his messages create a universal connection across our whole team.

One of the greatest game-day traditions at Notre Dame is attending Mass in the Basilica of the Sacred Heart before we walk to the stadium. It is the perfect opportunity to become grounded and vulnerable in our spirituality. I find it extremely valuable to have the opportunity to listen to Fr. Nate guide us through prayer a couple of hours before we focus on the task at hand on the field.

Following Mass, and just before our walk, Fr. Nate shares a prayer medal with everyone and explains why he has selected the saint represented on it. I always enjoy hearing about the values and characteristics of the saints he chooses because he makes a direct connection to where the team is on our journey at that moment. Because he is so embedded in our program, Fr. Nate can always find the perfect saint to share with us each week, which is one of the many attributes that makes him special.

One prayer medal I will never forget is the one presented for our national championship game in January 2025. With this game's extra significance, Fr. Nate upped his game and got us gold prayer medals! Following the game, Fr. Nate explained how that medal spoke to the moment:

> The Lord's Prayer asks for God's will to be done "on earth as it is in heaven." The medal for the championship game reflects God's love for each one of us in both realms. On one side: St. Michael the Archangel, our intercessor in heaven. Chief among the archangels, he is a courageous warrior who guards heaven and humanity against evil. We call on him to defend us in battles of every kind. He is the patron of soldiers, police officers, and other professions that face danger. The other side: a tangible manifestation of God's love for every one of us, a guardian angel. God's immense love for us isn't general or generic; it's focused on each of us through our guardian angels. The national championship medal is a reminder of that love and protection we have on earth and in heaven.

While we did not come out victorious in that game, we will not be denied—just delayed. Our fighting spirit continues!

As you follow along with *Pray Like a Champion Today*, it is my hope that you enjoy the stories of the experiences shared among our program and our team chaplain, Fr. Nate Wills.

Go Irish!

Marcus Freeman
Dick Corbett Head Football Coach
University of Notre Dame

INTRODUCTION

GRACE ON THE GRIDIRON

As the chaplain for the Notre Dame football team, the two most common questions I'm asked are "How did you become chaplain?" and "What do you actually *do* as chaplain?"

The answer to the first question is simple, and it's certainly not because of my extensive knowledge of the game of football. The priest who was the chaplain of the team before me, Fr. Mark Thesing, CSC, had taken on new responsibilities and decided it was time to enlist some help. He had a conversation with Fr. Pete McCormick, CSC, the director of Notre Dame's Campus Ministry, who is in charge of all of the chaplains, as to who might be a good fit for this role. The football chaplain is always a priest from the religious community that founded Notre Dame, the Congregation of Holy Cross, and they came up with my name. I got a phone call on a hot summer day in July 2018—Fr. Pete said that he had an unusual request for me and that I should feel free to say no. My mind was racing as to what he was going to ask me, figuring it was most likely to cover a Mass or Baptism. "We'd like you to consider being the chaplain to the Notre Dame football team," he said.

I was stunned. I remember exactly where I was on campus (walking through God Quad), and I recall standing there trying to find the logic in this request. *Why was I being asked to do this?* I played football for one year in high school, and I was . . . pretty bad. Ask any of my teammates. I was a marginal (at best!) defensive tackle with little understanding of the game and a light grasp on our playbook. I honestly didn't know that much about football, especially compared to some of my brothers in the Holy Cross community. We have priests and brothers in Holy Cross who have encyclopedic knowledge of football, and I'm not one of them. I've always been a Notre Dame fan and went to most of the games, but what made me qualified to be the team chaplain?

I gathered myself after a moment or two of silence and said, "Okay, two things, Pete. First of all, I'm honored. Thanks so much for thinking of me. Second . . . you know that I don't know that much about football, right?"

Fr. Pete responded in a measured voice, "Nate, we pay a lot of people a lot of money to know everything there is to know about football. We don't need you to call plays. We just need you to point them to Jesus."

Now *that* sounded like something I could do. Or at least *try* to do. So, I said yes, and that's how I became the chaplain.

As to the second question—"What do you actually *do* as chaplain?"—the answer is simple here too: not much! Of course, I mean that in the best way possible—everyone on the team has their job to do, and we're all expected to do it at the highest level. But when I'm not celebrating Mass with the team or cheering them on from the sidelines, there's a lot of waiting around. Away game weekends are especially uneventful for me because I follow the team's schedule during travel. Before the actual game, the team has a lot of position meetings but not a lot of commitments for me. But these in-between times of "waiting around" are some of my favorites.

Like the time we had to wait out a lightning storm during our 2023 game against NC State. I sat in a hallway with Coach

Freeman's wife, Joanna; recruiter Caleb Davis; and the assistant director of operations, Nina Baloun. We shared hearty laughs, great stories, and a lot of snacks.

It's when helmets aren't on and the clock isn't ticking that coaches and student-athletes can just be themselves. *That's* when conversations about things beyond football happen—like anyone, players and coaches and staff want someone to talk with about life and faith and the challenges we all face. Anyone in ministry will tell you that it's the in-between times that can be the most important, and I've certainly discovered life-giving connections by joking around with our police officers, praying with our flight attendants, and getting to know players or their parents. In my years with the team, I've witnessed some incredible moments of God's grace that never make a highlight reel or an NBC broadcast, from experiences that border on the miraculous to memorable conversations with coaches, staff members, walk-ons, refs, and fans. Some experiences have just made me smile. Other times I have been

moved to tears to see how God is at work in the lives of each one of us—even on the football field.

Over the years, I used some of the downtime on buses and planes to write down some of the details from these significant moments. I don't have a great memory (which makes me a bad friend but a *great* confessor!), so I knew if I didn't make note of them, I would soon forget some amazing moments of God's grace breaking through our day-to-day experience.

It started as a note on my iPhone titled "ND Football Chaplain" and then expanded to the stories you'll read in this book. I wrote some of the stories down immediately, as I could see how important they were right away. Others just seemed rather insignificant at the time only to reveal years later how God was at work. Some of the notes didn't make it into this book, but maybe they will yet prove grace-filled.

I often think my role as a Catholic priest is to participate in the prophetic tradition of St. John the Baptist. His life and mission were simple: to prepare the way of the Lord. When Jesus came walking right in front him and his followers, he did one simple thing: point. "There! There's the Lamb of God!" he said. "There's the one we've been waiting and longing for" (see John 1:35). A priest does the same thing in everyday life as he preaches about scripture passages and tries to relate them to our experiences. But sometimes when God's presence walks right in front of us, we have to just point. There! There's the presence of Jesus!

This book is an attempt to point out those moments where I have been privileged to see the grace of God walk right in front of me, sometimes even wearing a gold helmet. I've made a significant effort to make sure the people who are named in this book are okay with me telling these stories as well. My ministry as chaplain is based on trust, and I don't want to do anything to endanger that sacred bond. But I feel compelled to share the way I've witnessed God at work, even in places where some might not expect it. The stories here are a response to Jesus's call to "go into the whole world and proclaim the gospel to every creature" (Mark 16:15). And it's a chance to tell the stories of people who inspired me to want to be a better Christian and priest by their words, actions, faith, and witness. My hope is that they inspire you too.

CHAPTER 1

YOU'RE WITH US

Before my first home game, the previous football chaplain, Fr. Mark Thesing, CSC, gave me a three-page, single-spaced PDF of what to expect and what to do in this role. He's an exceptionally thoughtful and detailed person and covered nearly everything I would need to know for that first game—except for one thing: the player walk. He told me I was welcome to join the players, coaches, and staff as they walked from the football offices in the Guglielmino Athletics Complex (known affectionately as "the Gug") over to the locker room, which I happily did. But he didn't tell me what to expect *during* the walk.

The player walk is amazing. Fans and family line the sidewalk and cheer for the team as we walk by. The Notre Dame marching band stands on either side of the walk, energetically playing the Notre Dame fight song. One of my favorite parts of the experience is that as we walk past the band, I hear the

Scan the QR code or visit www.avemariapress.com/pages/pray-like-a-champion-today-resources to watch Manti Te'o address players on their walk to Notre Dame stadium to take on Cal in 2022.

different sections playing their parts—the warm harmonizing of the saxophones, the trills of the clarinets and piccolos, the low notes of the sousaphones, the bright chorus of the trumpets, and the effortless beat of the drummers, all working together to get the team fired up as they pass through a tunnel of sound.

Fans shout player names, yell play suggestions to the coaches (seriously, when I walk next to the offensive coordinator, I get an earful!), and every once in a while, I hear someone yell, "Let's go, Father!" It's absolutely exhilarating.

Amid all this excitement, I have to admit that I was pretty nervous about being part of this scene the first time I walked with the team. Who was *I* to be joining in this parade of jubilation? I wasn't about to go into battle the way our players were. I wasn't about to put my career on the line as our coaches were. I didn't feel as though I earned this honor, and I sure as heck didn't deserve to be cheered on any more than some random person off the street.

I often struggled with that same feeling of inadequacy during graduate school, and the momentousness of walking with the players past a sea of enthusiastic fans put me right back in it. My friend Frankie Jones likes to say that "imposter syndrome" should just be called "imposter phenomenon" because it is so widespread. Most of us are filled with doubts and insecurities as we go into the unknown, and I was certainly experiencing imposter phenomenon during the player walk at my first home game as chaplain.

A chorus of doubts was echoing through my head as I followed the team on this walk, and the doubts came to a crescendo as we neared the stadium. As the team walked in front of the Hesburgh Library, they split into two groups around the reflecting pond. I could see ahead as some went to the left and others went to the right. Each person seemed to know exactly where to go—except me. This wasn't in Fr. Mark's manual.

This mix of doubt and panic must have shown on my face because Mike Elston, our associate head coach and defensive line coach at the time, looked at me and said three simple words: "You're with us."

He nodded his head to the left, and with a huge sigh of relief, I joined him. I can't remember if he *actually* put his hand on my shoulder or if his words just had that effect. Either way, those three words were exactly *what* I needed to hear, exactly *when* I needed to hear them. It was a clear and unequivocal response to the chorus of doubts in my head—the silent taunts of being an imposter scattered into the darkness from whence they came.

I have often thought about the power of Coach Elston's three words: "You're with us." They offer assurance of

belonging and comfort, especially amid doubt and feeling like an outsider. If you're like me, when you're entering an unfamiliar context or community, you want to be accepted and welcomed. It's tough to feel as though you're alone and don't belong. For me, Coach Elston's words carry a spiritual weight.

Think of how the disciples must have felt after the Crucifixion when their best friend, mentor, teacher, and savior was suddenly gone. It must have been so disorienting to them to feel as though they had to start all over again. I'm sure darkness, doubt, and fear crept into their minds and hearts. In fact, toward the end of John's gospel, you can see the disciples panic when they meet uncertainty after Jesus's death and resurrection. The risen Jesus has appeared to them a couple times, but it's unclear what they're supposed to do next. In this doubt, Peter says, "I am going fishing," and the other disciples join him (John 21:3). When they were afraid and uncertain, these former fishermen went back to what was familiar and comfortable.

Matthew's gospel offers another perspective on this uncertain time when the resurrected Jesus appears to his disciples—he writes that "when they saw him, they worshiped, but they doubted" (28:17). In response to their doubt, Jesus offers these words of comfort: "Behold, I am with you always, until the end of the age." It's important to note that he doesn't say, "You shouldn't doubt!" or "Don't worry, everything is going to be fine!" He just says that through it all, he will be with them. Those are literally the last words of the Gospel of Matthew, and they echo the words at the *beginning* of Matthew's gospel: "They shall name him Emmanuel, which means 'God is with us.'" (1:23).

Jesus was born into the world because God loved us so much that he wanted to share every aspect of our humanity—to be *with us.* Through our baptism, God adopts us as his sons and daughters and changes our destiny through the gift of eternal life. By water and the Holy Spirit, God brings us into his family, essentially saying, "You're with us." Even though it can feel otherwise, we're never truly alone, and we always belong to the Christian family into which we have been adopted.

That day on my first player walk, it took one coach and three words to dispel the doubts that went through my head. It wasn't just a kind gesture—it was an invitation, and I took up a challenge to extend that invitation. How can I find ways to welcome people who might feel as though they're on the outside? How can I remind those in darkness and doubt that they're not alone? The reality is that we're *never* alone because in Jesus, Emmanuel, *God is with us.* He's always there, with his hand on our shoulder, pointing us in the right direction with the assuring words, "You're with us." Rest in that reality and listen to the crowds of heaven, cheering your name.

PRAY LIKE A CHAMPION

Today, pray for those who are lonely and feel like outsiders, that God might move us, his family, to open our arms to them as a sign of his special care for those who are lost.

CHOOSE
HARD

CHAPTER 2

CHOOSE HARD

On a snowy Friday morning in March 2023, I walked over from my room in Keough Hall to the Gug to put in my half hour on the elliptical while the guys worked out. As I was stowing my snowy shoes in a cubby and putting on my workout shoes, I caught sight of a coach who had just arrived. He made a bee line over to me and greeted me with a big bear hug. Offensive line coach Joe Rudolph and I had known each other for several years before I was chaplain to the Notre Dame football team. When I was in graduate school at the University of Wisconsin–Madison, Joe coached for the Badgers, and he and his wonderful family were parishioners at the parish where I lived. I was overjoyed that he was joining the team, and it was really great to reconnect with an old friend.

After my workout, I walked over to Joe and greeted a bunch of offensive linemen who were finishing their workout. I noticed the guys were wearing new gear: a simple blue Under Armour shirt with "NOTRE DAME FOOTBALL" on the front and two words in huge caps on the back, words I

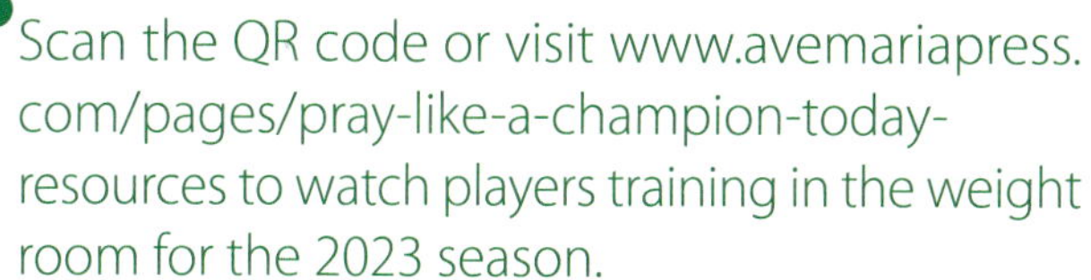

often find difficult to embrace, myself. The two words read simply, "CHOOSE HARD."

This was the first time I saw these words, but over the next several months and years, I would hear these words repeated again and again from coaches and players alike, using it as a rallying cry to make the tough decisions to do the right thing in building up our team. In this moment, on a snowy day in March, it was a reminder to our guys that these months of spring training are critically important for a successful season. The fact that they were written on the back of each of their shirts was an encouragement to go the extra mile, to not give up, and to practice the kind of grit and tenacity that lead to victory. Decisions on this everyday level build lifelong habits.

And these guys definitely need to encourage one another. I'm honestly not sure how the O-linemen do it. That's a

brutal and unrelenting position on the field that requires you to quickly assess a situation and then move decisively and strategically, all while holding your ground against an oncoming car crash. When the play is over, you do it again. And again.

O-linemen are constantly playing through pain and taping fingers or ankles so they can keep going. They also happen to be some of the most fun-loving, brilliant, faith-filled, and kind, gentle giants on our team. They're guys like the inquisitive and relentlessly hard-working Hunter Bivin and Tommy Kraemer. They're guys like Robert Hainsey—when I told him I was going to my first Tampa Bay Buccaneers game, he made sure that I had pre-game field passes and interrupted his warm-ups to give me a big hug. They're guys like Blake Fisher and Tosh Baker who are always smiling. I'm pretty sure I have never once walked past any of those guys without

them reaching out for a fist-bump. They're guys who choose hard every day.

Those two words stuck with me, and I appreciate their simple yet challenging message. It has come with a personal realization as well: I struggle to "choose hard." I'm much more likely to choose the ease of a text message rather than calling someone. There are times when I could offer a gentle nudge to a family member, but instead I opt out of potential conflict. I often struggle to be attentive in long pastoral conversations and find myself avoiding tasks that require deep attention.

I suppose it's comforting to know I'm not alone. Jesus encourages his disciples to "strive to enter through the narrow gate, for many, I tell you, will attempt to enter but will not be strong enough" (Luke 13:24). And Paul's Letter to the Romans is chock-full of encouragements to "choose hard," even as he admits that he doesn't do the good he wants to do and that he does the evil he doesn't want to do (Romans 7:19). Still, St. Paul encourages the early Christian community in Rome to persevere in striving to pattern their life after Christ Jesus. Intentionally embracing hard work and battling against our inclinations toward comfort and ease has always been a struggle—this challenge echoes through the centuries.

To be clear, I'm not suggesting that we should manufacture ways to make our lives more difficult or that living the Christian life requires giving up *everything* that makes our lives easier. I am simply saying that taking the easy way out will not break us out of our comfort zones and lead to growth.

The early followers of Jesus faced this question in a defining moment in John's gospel. Jesus tells the crowd, "I am the living bread that came down from heaven; whoever eats this bread will live forever; and the bread that I will give is my flesh for the life of the world" (John 6:51). It is a surprising revelation—one that is difficult to comprehend—and people leave.

They're uneasy with this language, which makes having faith more demanding. The crowd liked Jesus better when he was multiplying loaves and fishes earlier in this chapter, or when he was healing the sick. But this? Believing Jesus here takes real faith. And when things get challenging, the crowds start to drift. Even the disciples say, "This saying is hard; who can accept it?" (John 6:60).

When we hit difficult moments in our lives, it's tempting to echo their reaction. But our faith calls us to beliefs and actions that invite us to *choose hard*. And whether that's theological truths beyond our understanding, the moral teachings of the Church, or our faith tradition's stance on social justice issues, we also will have to face a difficult decision: Do I follow the crowd that walks away from Jesus? Or do I stay, standing with the disciples in faith and in steadfast friendship with him?

Jesus asks the Twelve directly, "Do you also want to leave?" And Peter courageously and beautifully speaks up at this moment: "Master, to whom shall we go? You have the words of eternal life!" (John 6:67–68).

Each of us, at some point in our journey, will face doubt or fear or frustration in our Christian faith, and we will have to answer Jesus's question: Will you leave with the rest of the crowd? Will you look elsewhere for fulfillment and an easier way? Or can you stand fast with the Lord? Can you and I, by the grace of God, *choose hard*?

We come together to pray and worship because we need each other to respond to the challenge of faith. For Catholics, we come together for the celebration of the Mass to be strengthened by this community of believers, to be inspired by God's word in our scriptures, and to be fortified by Christ's body and blood to live the Christian life week after week, day after day. When we fail, we seek God's mercy and try to amend our lives. And with the tenacity of an O-lineman, when the day is over, we tape up our knuckles and do it again. And again.

We Christians are invited to choose the "narrow door," which means following the pattern of our Lord Jesus in compassion, sacrificial love, and service that will lead to the glory of eternal life with God in heaven.

In my religious community, there's a saying in our rule of life, the Constitutions of the Holy Cross: "If we shirk the cross, gone too will be our hope." There is no shortcut to the resurrection. One of the few guarantees of the Christian life is that it will involve facing and enduring the cross in some way. But suffering is not the end of the story.

Scan the QR code or visit www.tinyurl.com/holy-cross-constitutions to read the Constitutions of Holy Cross.

Our offensive linemen *choose hard* in order to achieve "team glory," as Coach Freeman likes to put it. We Christians *choose hard* so that we can join the inevitable challenges, sufferings, and setbacks of life to the Cross of Christ. There, by more deeply depending on God and surrendering our egos and selfishness, we receive the grace of new life.

It's not easy, but I am convinced that if you want to realize your dreams in this life and experience eternal life with Christ in heaven in the next, there's only one path: choose hard.

PRAY LIKE A CHAMPION

Today, pray for those who struggle to entrust their lives to God, that deeper faith, hope, and love might strengthen them to persevere in difficulty and trust in God's goodness.

PRAY
FOR
US
FOR
US
ST. JOAN OF ARC
JOAN OF AR

CHAPTER 3

A BATTLE-READY TRADITION

Here at Notre Dame, we often joke that if you do something twice, it's a tradition—so you better not change it! One of my absolute favorite traditions involves giving holy medals depicting different saints to student-athletes before every game.

I first learned about this tradition from my brother, who was on the ND basketball team. He collected all of the pre-game medals he was given and eventually strung them together and made a (very heavy and very large) rosary for my grandmother. So I knew this tradition existed since at least the 1990s but had no idea how far back it stretched.

When Fr. Mark was first showing me the ropes of being the football chaplain, he told me about the tradition of giving holy medals to the players. Over the years, he had built a spreadsheet that listed all of the saints we had asked for prayer since 2010. On it, I could see he had created a five-year rotation of the medals so that players wouldn't get duplicates during their career. He told me that at the end of the team Mass, he would tell everyone a bit about the life of the saint depicted on the medals, bless them, and then hand them out to the players and coaches.

What players do with the medals is entirely up to them. Some keep them in their locker, some wear them on a chain around their neck, and one player told me that he always gives them to his girlfriend. Our faith-filled and very successful kicker for the 2021 season, Jon Doerer, always affixed the holy medal to his shoe during the game and then added the medal to the chain that he wore around his neck. Our former athletic director told me that he kept all of the holy medals from the games in his desk, but, he said, "I have two drawers: one for the winners and one for the losers." I nearly doubled over in laughter!

I then told him that they were *all* winners since they had been canonized as saints and were, therefore, with Christ in heaven! After some good-natured discussion, we agreed that some saints might have more intercessory power for football

than others. For example, the holy medal for the 2023 loss against Marshall was Our Lady of Guadalupe, and the one for the 2024 loss against Northern Illinois University was St. Rose of Lima—perhaps these great saints from Mexico and Peru mistakenly filed our prayers under *fútbol* instead of "American football."

Because some players wear the holy medals during the game, Fr. Mark told me they had to be battle-ready. This meant that the flimsy medal loop at the top of each of the medals wouldn't suffice. He explained that he didn't want the loop to pull apart or break and fall off during the game, so he came up with a clever—if painstaking—solution: He removed the little metal ring on every medal and replaced it with a 7 mm split ring. You know, the kind of coiled ring you have on your keychain—the one you have to pry open when you want to add a key? Yeah, like that—only really, really tiny. Fr. Mark purchased specialized pliers with a little tooth on it to open the split ring so he could then attach it to the holy medal. It's a great idea, except when you have to do it literally thousands of times. We order 200 medals for every home game and 150 for every away game.

Replacing these tiny rings is one of the hidden, behind-the-scenes tasks of being a part of this program, similar to the student managers who mix two types of Gatorade to create a special "Gameday Green" flavor for every game, or the stadium ushers who arrive three hours before home games to do a security sweep. I've gotten quicker, but it's a task that takes time every week. I decided to spend some of that time praying over the medals and sometimes listening to audio histories of the saint so that I can tell players about their life. Other times, my process isn't quite so edifying and I end up watching reruns of *The Office*.

After I bless the medals and distribute the medals to the players and coaches, there are usually some left over. I keep them in a little black pouch in my pocket and give them out to various people on the sidelines: student equipment managers, sports medicine professionals, our police officers, the refs, and our team doctors. I love telling them a little about the saint and if there's a particular reason why that saint is appropriate for that game.

I took over as the sole football chaplain for the 2020 season and remember having an energetic conversation with friends one evening about how much I liked this tradition and wanted to find a way to connect with Notre Dame fans who might want to know who the saint of the game was. Fr. Pete McCormick, CSC, is chaplain of the men's basketball team and encouraged me to post them on Instagram. I actually had created an account in March of 2019, @PrayLikeAChampionToday, but I didn't know what to post on it. With the enthusiastic encouragement of my friends, I shared a picture of my hand holding the holy medal for our first game that season. I gave it this exceptionally brief caption: "Every game we give our players, coaches, and staff a holy medal. Today's: St. John the Baptist. 'I must decrease that Christ may increase' (John 3:30)."

I wanted to do something more than just post a picture of me holding the medal, so I started taking photos of players holding the medals and tagging their accounts. The first time I did this was for the 2020 Florida State game, and Xavier Watts kindly held the medal. Eventually, I started adding multiple

Scan the QR code or visit www.instagram.com/praylikeachampiontoday to follow the Pray Like a Champion Today account on Instagram.

photos and showing the holy medal first and then the player who was holding it.

I mixed things up at times and asked celebrities or alums to hold the medal. I got NFL Hall of Famers Tim Brown and Jerome Bettis to hold the medals at our 2022 Shamrock Series game in Las Vegas. It has been really fun to enlist the help of so many different people—from our mascot, the Leprechaun, to astronaut (and ND parent) Col. Mike Hopkins; from walk-ons to star players.

My descriptions of the life of the saint on the holy medal kept getting longer until eventually I discovered the character limit for an Instagram post. These posts have become an opportunity to share the remarkable lives of these saints, to feature our student-athletes, and to preach the Gospel. A perfect combination, in my humble opinion.

In his book *The University of Notre Dame: A History*, historian Fr. Tom Blantz, CSC, tells the story of the first recorded instance of Notre Dame student-athletes receiving holy medals: October 13, 1923, when the Notre Dame football team played Army in Brooklyn, New York. West Point had asked Hollywood star Elsie Janis to do a ceremonial kickoff, and in response, beloved Holy Cross priest John Francis O'Hara (who was later elevated to cardinal) told the football team that if the cadets had this Hollywood star on their side, St. Joan of Arc would be on our side. He handed out holy medals of the great soldier-saint to the players who went on to win the game 13–0.

Cardinal O'Hara continued to distribute medals of the saints for the remainder of his time at Notre Dame, and one of Fr. Blantz's historical references claimed that "press coverage of this practice helped popularize, particularly among Catholic boys, the wearing of medals during sports events."

Providentially, a friend pointed that passage out to me as he read Fr. Blantz's book in the summer of 2023. On October 14, 2023, one hundred years and one day later after Cardinal O'Hara started the practice, Notre Dame played Southern Cal at home. The timing was perfect, and it was too good to pass up: I gave the team St. Joan of Arc medals at the end of Mass in the Basilica of the Sacred Heart, where Cardinal O'Hara is buried.

While college football continues to change, this long-standing tradition reveals something about the unique place Notre Dame occupies in this sport. We don't confine our faith and values to a church building—we carry them to everything we do, even on the football field. Every challenge we face is an opportunity to look to the lives of the saints for inspiration and courage and assistance in following Jesus. Giving holy medals to student-athletes is part of a wider tradition of faithfulness that has been handed on to us from generations past, and it's our duty and honor to continue to pass them along to those who will come after us.

It was thrilling to honor the great Notre Dame tradition of giving out holy medals of this same great soldier-saint to our team one century later. Her intercession of courage in battle inspired the 1923 Notre Dame team to a victory over Army, and I'd like to think she had a hand in our game one hundred years later: We beat Southern Cal 48–20.

PRAY LIKE A CHAMPION

Today, pray for those who desire to hand faith on to the next generation, that, along with the saints, they might provide a compelling witness to God's life-giving love. (Also, pray that we beat Southern Cal this year!)

Scan the QR code or visit www.avemariapress.com/pages/pray-like-a-champion-today-resources to watch behind-the-scenes highlights from the 2023 victory over Southern Cal.

BOWL
2023

CHAPTER 4

HE'S OUR GUY

One Tuesday in February 2022, I was on my way to the grocery store, and I decided on a whim to stop at the football building. There was nothing going on in the player lounge, nobody in the media room (where fun and fantastic creative projects are often brewing), so I went upstairs to the coaches' offices. As I walked down the hallway, I could see a light was on in Hunter Bivin's office—he was director of player development at the time. As I got closer, I could see he was talking to Coach Freeman.

They greeted me warmly, and Coach Freeman asked if I had met the new defensive coaches. I told him that I had met Al Washington, but that was it so far. We had just hired a number of new defensive coaches, including a new defensive coordinator, Al Golden. He was here in the building, gathered with his new staff. I was surprised to hear this news because it was Tuesday, and he had just been coaching the Cincinnati Bengals linebackers on Sunday—at the Super Bowl.

He told me they were all gathered in the defensive coordinator room down the hall and I should go say hello. I said great and turned to go.

He stopped me. "Wait, Fr. Nate. Lemme take you over there and introduce you to the guys."

I said, "Coach, I'm fine. I'm a priest—I meet new people all the time!" I told him that I knew he was busy and it was no big deal.

He didn't agree; he didn't argue. He just said, "Come with me."

We walked down the hall together and he introduced me to the new coaches. I already knew Chris O'Leary and Mike Mickens, but Al Golden and the rest of his coaches were all new to the program.

I had read a bit about Coach Golden on my news feed the day before, but I didn't really know what to expect. He was tall, confident, and had a kind smile as I shook his hand.

I'm not sure what was going through my head next, but for all the assurances I had *just* made to Coach Freeman about being comfortable meeting new people, I managed to blurt out to Coach Golden, "It's nice to meet you! I've seen you on . . . you know . . . the internet!"

He chuckled, and I told them that I was the chaplain of the football team. Coach Freeman clapped me on the shoulder and said to the coaches, "He's our guy." With a couple more pleasantries, I went on my way to the grocery store.

Somewhere between the produce aisle and the frozen section of the grocery store, the importance of what just happened occurred to me. One of the most challenging parts of my first couple of months—okay, years—with the team was building trust. It seems as though everyone (EVERYONE!) wants something from our student athletes and coaches. Even when players live in dorms on campus, they are often asked, "Can you please sign this? Can I take a selfie?" It's all well-intentioned and may even be exciting for the student-athletes, but it can lead to skepticism about whom they can trust and who just wants something from them.

Coming into a new building and a new program as Coach Golden and the other coaches were, there is a frenzy of new people to meet. A natural reaction to this novel environment might be one of caution: Whom do I trust? Who has my best interest in mind, and who is playing political games? Where can I go when things are difficult, and who wants to get to know me as a person?

It must be particularly difficult for players and coaches who are not Catholic to know what to think about this priest who randomly shows up in the offseason and hangs out on the sidelines during games. Let's face it—pop culture rarely paints priests in a positive light.

All of this made what Coach Freeman had just done for me even more important and significant. Instead of letting me walk into that room by myself and say hello, he offered an *authorization*. Introducing me to that group of guys was an endorsement: This guy is okay. He's trustworthy. He's "our guy." It was an exceptionally kind and hospitable thing to do, and it wouldn't be the last time Coach Freeman did this for me.

Right after our portal transfer students arrived in January 2023, I ran into Coach Freeman in the Gug. He told me the new transfers, including Sam Hartman and Javontae Jean-Baptiste, were gathered in the auditorium and I should go say hi. I agreed and headed that way. Twenty seconds later, I heard someone running down the hall behind me. Coach Freeman caught up with me and said that he wanted to introduce them to me personally.

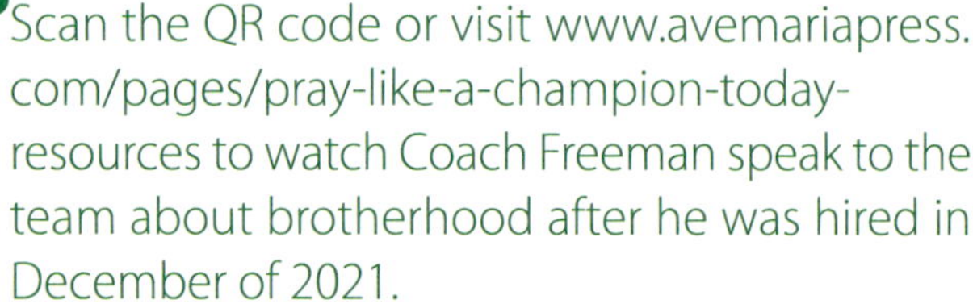

Scan the QR code or visit www.avemariapress.com/pages/pray-like-a-champion-today-resources to watch Coach Freeman speak to the team about brotherhood after he was hired in December of 2021.

This kind of authorization has really helped me build trust with the guys in our program. It's what friends do for each other, it's often how business networking works, and it's even how people meet their future spouses. I can't help but think that this is the way true evangelization happens as well.

In the very first chapter of John's gospel, the apostle Andrew is following John the Baptist when John points to Jesus and says, "Behold, the Lamb of God" (1:29). Here's the one we've been looking for! he is saying—this is the one we've been waiting for! Follow him. And immediately, Andrew does. He has a conversation with Jesus and spends time with him that day, presumably listening, building trust, and determining if he truly is the Messiah. Sometime after (John isn't specific), Andrew goes and gets his brother Simon Peter. He tells him simply, "We have found the Messiah" (1:41), and Peter leaves his fishing nets and follows after Jesus.

Andrew *authorized* Jesus to Simon Peter. Andrew told him that this stranger was trustworthy, that this was the Anointed

One, and that they needed to follow him and leave everything else behind. Two thousand years later, I think this kind of endorsement is often the most effective means of sharing our faith in Jesus. Some people come to a moment of conversion through reading some great spiritual classic. Others find the Lord through life experiences that bring them to their knees. But for most of us, coming to know and love Jesus happens through *authorization*. It comes from someone we know and trust telling us that they have found the Messiah, the One who satisfies the deepest longing of their heart, the missing piece who makes this entire journey here on earth make sense.

We're called to be authorizers of Jesus: our friend, brother, savior, and Lord. In a world that can be skeptical and cautious about faith in general, and Catholicism in particular, people need to know that we have found treasure in a relationship with Jesus, that we have found peace in Christ's presence in the Eucharist, and that we have found inspiration in the lives of the saints throughout salvation history. Jesus invites Andrew with the words, "Come and see," and he's speaking to us too—we're called to follow after him and to invite others along the journey. When they know of our love and see the difference faith makes in our lives, others will join as well, knowing that we all come to Jesus because "he's our guy."

PRAY LIKE A CHAMPION

Today, pray for those who are searching for meaning and purpose, that God might place someone in their life who can lead them through word and deed to deeper faith.

NOTRE DAME FIGHTING IRISH
T.O.L 3
0
1ST 2:48
BALL ON
0
T.O.L 3
SOUTH CAROLINA GAMECOCKS
55
52

CHAPTER 5

NO BAD DAYS

During the football season, I try to drop by practice once a week or so. I don't do much other than offer a lot of chucks on the shoulders and greetings to student-athletes, managers, staff members, and coaches, but I still like to do it. Usually, one of my first stops is to go give an encouraging word to the guys who are injured over in the area that's affectionately called "the pit." This is where anyone who is injured works out during practice. That's right—if you're hurt or injured but can still manage, you still come to practice and work out. And let me tell you, it's not a nice place to be.

The workouts in the pit are grueling. While the other players on the team are running routes and playing the game they love, these guys are going as fast as they can for a minute straight on one of those bikes that has a big fan and arm rowers. Then they head over to do arm waves with heavy ropes for another timed period. These athletes are on the team because they love playing football, and the combination of not being able to play and having to do a particularly intense workout is rough.

Recently, I took a small group of Catholic school principals to the football weight room, where they witnessed two guys leaving practice with their legs in boots and driving small scooters out the door of the weight room. They were dripping with sweat. "Did they make those guys lift?!" one of the principals asked me.

I said, "Well, yeah. It's just their legs that are injured." As it came out of my mouth, I recognized how cruel that sounded. But it's also the reality of training and playing on an elite football program that to be ready to return to play, injured student-athletes need to maintain their fitness.

Two days before the Clemson game in 2022, I decided to stop by practice. It was an evening practice, and I saw one of the guys who instantly brought a smile to my face, Bo Bauer. Bo lived in my same dorm, Keough Hall, for several years. For his entire sophomore year, every time Bo saw me in the dorm, he would give me a big, enthusiastic, golden-retriever-energy

hug. One time, I was coming down the stairs in Keough and he was coming up, and he greeted me with less of a hug and more of a tackle, nearly sending me flying down the steps.

At practice that day in 2022, Bo had his foot propped up on his scooter because of a recent injury. As ever, he had a big smile on his face. He shook my hand, and I asked him how he was doing.

"Great!" he said. I believed him. He was always so positive and upbeat, and not in a phony way. He asked how things were in the dorm, and I gave him a brief update on some of the guys and the latest goings-on.

I was struck by his optimism in that moment and asked him how he had such a great attitude all the time. I didn't expect the answer he gave.

He told me about his best friend from high school who was a star wrestler and was going to possibly make it to the Olympics. Then one match, as he picked a guy up and moved to pin him, his friend's neck twisted at an odd angle and broke. From that moment on, his friend was a quadriplegic. Experiencing this moment with his friend fundamentally changed the way that Bo saw the world.

His friend had a saying that he shared with Bo: "No bad days." That was Bo's frame of reference for facing life's challenges: no bad days. It's a beautiful way of looking into the face of difficult moments and perceived setbacks with gratitude and resilience, never giving in to the temptation to just dismiss an entire day as "bad." I was so impressed at the way this young man faced an obstacle like his injury with such a mature perspective.

This insight and ability to reframe challenges—even tragedies—was a choice that both Bo and his friend made after his accident. It was something of a pact, a phrase that they often used to lift up each other in discouraging moments. Choosing to reframe difficult moments of our lives is such a powerful way to move us from the passenger's seat of self-pity and victimhood to the driver's seat of acceptance and ownership. It's an exceptionally difficult thing to do and takes a ton of resolve, faith, and support from others who are unwilling to let you falter.

We can take some consolation that this type of reframing was difficult even for the saints! In one of the most powerful passages from St. Paul's letters, he writes about receiving "a thorn in the flesh." He asks God to remove it, but to no avail:

> A thorn in the flesh was given to me, an angel of Satan, to beat me, to keep me from being too elated. Three times I begged the Lord about this, that it might leave me, but he said to me, "My grace is sufficient for you, for power is made perfect in weakness." I will rather boast most gladly of my weaknesses, in order that the power of Christ may dwell with me.
>
> Therefore, I am content with weaknesses, insults, hardships, persecutions, and constraints, for the sake of Christ; for when I am weak, then I am strong. (2 Corinthians 12:7–10)

St. Paul heard God telling him that this difficulty—this thorn—wasn't something he was going to take away. Instead, God was using it as an invitation to rely more fully on his grace and find the strength that comes from God alone. God's message to Paul—that "power is made perfect in weakness"—is counterintuitive for us. Humans have been obsessed with power throughout our existence, yet the truth of this insight echoes through the millennia: It's often only in the moments when our own strength fails that we're able to look to God and let his grace supply what we cannot.

St. Paul never explains what his "thorn" actually *is*, and I think that's part of the power of this passage. That ambiguity invites us to consider our own thorns—past regrets, current difficulties, or future longings—that we would like for God to remove from our lives. But that's not how it worked for St. Paul, and it's likely not how it works for most of us. Instead, we have to make a choice, as Bo and his friend did: resent or reframe. We can either remain stuck in the resentments that keep us from moving forward, or embrace our weaknesses as St. Paul did, trusting that the thorns in our lives can actually help draw us closer to Jesus.

The Holy Cross Constitutions proclaim this hope in Jesus: "There is no failure the Lord's love cannot reverse, no humiliation he cannot exchange for blessing, no anger he cannot dissolve, no routine he cannot transfigure. All is swallowed up in victory" (118).

That day at practice, with his foot resting on his scooter, Bo told me the end of his friend's story: He graduated at the top of his undergraduate class and went on to Harvard Law School. Bo then said rather matter-of-factly that his injury would take a year to heal. But he wasn't looking for pity or even sympathy. He said it almost as a way of telling me, "Don't worry, I'll be back." He even made fun of himself as he poked his finger into the quad of his injured leg and said, "See how

Scan the QR code or visit www.avemariapress.com/pages/pray-like-a-champion-today-resources to watch a hype video from the 2022 season narrated by Bo Bauer.

squishy this is? Compared to this one?" And he flexed his right quad to a tight defined muscle. "It turns to jelly so fast!" he chuckled.

He never stopped smiling. After all, like yesterday, today, and tomorrow, Bo was having a good day.

PRAY LIKE A CHAMPION

Today, pray for those who are suffering from injury or illness, that God might give them resilience and hope.

23
1988
1977

CHAPTER 6

THE LOCKER ROOM CRUCIFIX

Practice is fascinating. At first it can seem like a hive of bees. Players are in constant motion, and coaches are teaching, encouraging, and sometimes barking commands. But when you observe the patterns behind the activity, it becomes more like a well-choreographed dance—everybody seems to know where they're going and what they're up to. One minute they'll run a play; the next minute players are doing drills. A whistle blows, and they all run to one side of the field. Another whistle, and they're running plays again. Equipment managers are snagging balls, and sports medicine students are slinging water bottles. There's a beautiful rhythm to it all, and I often just stand in awe of the incredible coordination it all takes.

Most practices take place in our Irish Athletics Center, or IAC. It's an amazing place—a state-of-the-art indoor practice field with beautiful high ceilings and even a giant "play like a champion" sign! The players just call the IAC "the Indoor," and it is honestly one of my favorite places on campus. It's not air-conditioned, but it has a bunch of garage doors that roll up for easy access to the two outdoor playing fields we use.

One day at practice, I was standing with Eric King, who is in charge of all football facilities at Notre Dame. He's a faithful Catholic and has been with the program for a long time. And he always has an encouraging word or something kind to say. As I stood with Eric, I looked around the IAC and noticed something was missing.

Every classroom at Notre Dame has a crucifix. When I was an undergraduate at Notre Dame, my fellow college seminarians and I would play the game of who could spot the crucifix first in every classroom we entered. Without fail, it was there. The presence of this ordinary symbol might seem like a small thing, but I don't think it is. It says a lot about this place that wherever you go on campus, you see the ultimate reason for everything we do: to proclaim Jesus to the world.

I asked Eric where the crucifix was in the IAC. He and I scanned the whole facility and couldn't find one. He said, "We gotta fix that!" That's all I needed to hear.

It just took a little bit of asking around to find out that there's an office, the Notre Dame Sacristy Supply office, that has an entire collection of older crucifixes with every size and shape you could imagine. When I saw the collection and was asked which one I wanted, I felt as though I was in that scene from *Indiana Jones and the Last Crusade* where Indy has to choose which cup is the Holy Grail in a room full of chalices. I picked a fairly modestly sized one and brought it to Eric. The two of us excitedly looked around the Indoor with one question in mind: "Now where do we put it?" We came up with a couple of options, and a week later, he sent me a text and told me I should come by to see it.

As Eric and I walked in, I saw it right away. The crucifix hung at eye-level on one of the more prominent walls in the Indoor. It was perfect. Then I looked right below it to see that the crucifix had been mounted above the automated external

defibrillator (AED). I laughed out loud, chucked Eric on the arm, and said, “Look! Two life-saving devices on one wall!”

A crucifix is different from a simple cross because it has the body of Jesus on it, which is called the *corpus*. The word “crucifix” comes from the two Latin words, *cruci* and *fixus*, meaning “(one) fixed to a cross.” While the body of Jesus is often stylized or painted on a crucifix, it is definitely still recognizable as a man, tortured and dying.

I have often wondered how a crucifix might look to someone unfamiliar with the story of the life, death, and resurrection of Jesus. No doubt they might think it was a bit strange to decorate a classroom with the image of a man bloodied and dying on an ancient Roman torture device. Yet this is the most profound symbol of hope in our Christian faith.

Crucifixion was, by design, an inefficient way of killing someone. The purpose of crucifying criminals and revolutionaries was to hoist them high so all the people could see them suffer—the crucified served as a reminder to all onlookers of what would happen to you if you challenged Roman authority. It was meant to be a public symbol of shame, fear, torture, intimidation, and deadly consequences. The message was clear: Stay down, be afraid, and if you rise up, this is what awaits you—a humiliating and painful death on a cross.

The resurrection of Jesus changed all of that.

Christians began to claim the image of the Crucified as a symbol of victory over something much bigger than the Roman authorities—it became a symbol of Jesus's victory over sin and death. What once stood for fear and oppression now became a sign of liberation, courage, and transformation. So we proudly display it in our homes, our churches, and even on the wall of the IAC.

There's another very special and unique crucifix related to Notre Dame football that not many people get to see; even fewer know its significance. It's a crucifix that dates back to the time of Knute Rockne, Notre Dame's legendary football player-turned-coach. (I feel the need to gently correct how you may have just read that. Over time, many have lost the way that Rockne's friends, family, and players would have

"I'VE GOT TO GO, ROCK. IT'S ALL RIGHT.
I'M NOT AFRAID. SOMETIME, ROCK,
WHEN THE TEAM'S UP AGAINST IT,
WHEN THINGS ARE WRONG AND THE
BREAKS ARE BEATING THE BOYS...
TELL THEM TO GO IN THERE WITH ALL
THEY'VE GOT AND WIN JUST ONE FOR
THE GIPPER. I DON'T KNOW WHERE I'LL
BE THEN, ROCK, BUT I'LL KNOW ABOUT
IT, AND I'LL BE HAPPY."

pronounced his first name. The *K* is not silent, so it isn't pronounced "NOOT"; it's "kuh-NOOT.")

In the home locker room inside of Notre Dame Stadium hangs the crucifix, mounted on two pieces of aged wood, one broken at the bottom. Just below it there's a plaque that recounts the famous dying words of Notre Dame's first All-American, George Gipp, to his coach, Knute Rockne:

> I've got to go, Rock. It's all right. I'm not afraid. Sometime, Rock, when the team's up against it, when things are wrong and the breaks are beating the boys . . . tell them to go in there with all they've got and win just one for the Gipper. I don't know where I'll be then, Rock, but I'll know about it, and I'll be happy.

The commonly held belief is that the wood of that cross is from a broken fence—a fence from a farm in Chase County, Kansas, that was broken as the plane Knute Rockne was traveling on crashed to the earth. Together, one could think of the plaque and the wooden cross as simply memorials to tragic losses for the Notre Dame family—Gipp was only twenty-five years old when he died of pneumonia; Rockne's death at only forty-three left a wife and four children behind. But the crucifix on top of the fence-post cross mounted above Gipp's words reminds all who look upon it that death does not have the final word because of Jesus's victory of redemption on the Cross.

Scan the QR code or visit www.avemariapress.com/pages/pray-like-a-champion-today-resources to watch a video tour of Notre Dame Stadium and its history.

My religious community, the Congregation of Holy Cross, claims as its motto *Ave Crux spes unica*, a Latin phrase that means "Hail the Cross, our only hope." Bearing the cross in the Christian life will certainly look different for each one of us. The Holy Cross Constitutions speak to this reality beautifully:

> Whether it be unfair treatment, fatigue or frustration at work, a lapse of health, tasks beyond talents, seasons of loneliness, bleakness in prayer, the aloofness of friends; or whether it be the sadness of our having inflicted any of this on others . . . there will be dying to do on our way to the Father. (117)

Whatever our crosses look like in life, faith invites us to rest in the reality that no present darkness is greater than the light of Christ and the promise of the resurrection. God sends us signs of his love to strengthen our faith—signs that can be as simple as a crucifix hanging on the wall, which reminds us that the transformative power of the Cross of Jesus is our only hope.

PRAY LIKE A CHAMPION

Today, pray for those who struggle to bear the crosses that have been laid on their shoulders, that God might reveal to them the promise of new life that he sent his Son to bring us.

CHAPTER 7

MEN IN BLACK

In the midst of the 2020 COVID season, we played Pitt at Heinz Field. It was a fun game—mostly because we won big, but also because it was fall 2020 and I actually got to *do* something amid the pandemic quarantine. Everything was locked down, sterilized, and awful that fall . . . except for football.

I spoke at length about the tradition of giving holy medals to our student-athletes in chapter 3, and I mentioned that I always order some extra medals to give out on the sidelines of the games. In particular, I like giving holy medals to the referees. (*No*, it's not to influence the outcome of the game or to proselytize. And it's only a coincidence that we're wearing similar black-and-white uniforms.)

The holy medals are a unique Notre Dame tradition, and I have had dozens of refs show me the medals that I gave them in past seasons or games. I've seen holy medals hanging on their whistles, tucked inside their small refereeing notebooks, or dutifully zipped away in pockets. Several refs have independently told me about a game several years ago when a head ref got to the moment of the coin toss at the beginning of the game and realized he didn't have a coin. But he did have a holy medal. He showed the players which side was heads and which was tails, and by golly, he flipped it in the air to start the game. "But, Father," one of the refs who told me this story assured me with a smile, "he didn't let it hit the ground."

Nearly to a person, college football refs are fantastic people. They are funny, smart, and energetic. Also, almost no one talks to the refs before the game, so I have made a practice of saying hello to them and chatting a little bit. Most college refs have careers during the week as well, and I have been fascinated to hear about their lives as teachers, funeral home directors, firefighters, engineers, programmers, principals, and just about any other career you might imagine.

They're fascinating people and often deeply faith-filled. In fact, at one game in 2020, the head ref called me over to pray with his crew. I remember another ref who, when I gave him one of the team's holy medals for the week, looked down at the medal in his hand, thanked me, and looked up with tears in his eyes. He said that his wife was very sick and that he was going to give the holy medal to her. He told me her name, and I asked him if we could pray together for her. With a relieved look, said, "*Yes*."

So back to the Pitt game during the pandemic: That particular week's medal depicted St. John Paul II (whose feast fell just two days before the game). I gave out medals to most of the refs at Pitt, but one in particular was overjoyed as he received it. He told me that he wasn't Catholic but that his faith in God was really important to him. He thanked me profusely and said, "Hey! Check this out."

Scan the QR code or visit www.avemariapress.com/pages/pray-like-a-champion-today-resources to watch highlights from the 2020 victory over Pitt.

He unbuttoned the top buttons of his shirt and pulled back his striped jersey with both hands like Superman to reveal a black T-shirt underneath that said, in big white letters, "Psalm 91." He began reciting this, and I joined in as we said it together:

> You who dwell in the shelter of the Most High,
> who abide in the shade of the Almighty,
> Say to the Lord, "My refuge and fortress,
> my God in whom I trust."

His eyes widened, and he was clearly impressed that a Catholic could recite sacred scripture from memory! I didn't have the heart to tell him that his particular psalm just happens to be the one priests pray for night prayer every Sunday, so I have been reciting it since I was in seminary. I wish I knew all of sacred scripture that well!

Psalm 91 is also a psalm I have used in the hospital with people who have been sick, struggling, or even near death. It's a psalm of deep faith that reminds us who God is, how he will deliver us from our foes, and his promise of protection for us all.

Reciting that psalm together was a great moment of connection between us. It was clearly important to both of us, and as we recited it, it was like finding out that we shared a mutual friend, grew up in the same town, or were somehow distant cousins. It was a special moment of connection through the words of sacred scripture and reminded me of the grace that can happen if we put ourselves and our faith out there for others to see—whether with the Roman collar I wear on the sidelines or his Psalm 91 T-shirt.

This moment also encouraged me to be bolder in inviting others into our beautiful Catholic traditions—to integrate my own faith in a way that shines more brightly through the things I do and say. It was an unexpected moment to encounter his faith on the field and to celebrate our brotherhood in Christ. It also made me wonder how many opportunities like that I miss by assuming that someone doesn't want to talk about faith or (more likely) because I just don't bother to take a conversation in that direction. I hope God will continue to use encounters like this to give me courage and remind me what happens when I share my faith with others—even the refs.

\\\\\\\\\\

PRAY LIKE A CHAMPION

Today, pray for those who lack meaningful relationships, that God might encourage them with authentic and faithful friends.

\\\\\\\\\\

TRAIN LIKE
A CHAMPION
TODAY
FIGHTING IRISH
FIGHTING IRISH
FIGHTING IRISH

CHAPTER 8

THE 11TH COMMANDMENT

After my first season with the team, I started thinking about ways I could be more present to the guys throughout the off-season in the spring semester. Between that and my desire to drop about twenty pounds, I emailed our strength and conditioning coach, Matt Balis, to ask if he would mind if I worked out in the Gug some mornings while the team was there. I could say hi to the guys and get a workout in. Win-win!

Coach Balis had a quick and enthusiastic response: "I think it would be awesome if you were around here to work out and get to be around the guys more." I was pumped! I immediately texted my brother to tell him that, ahem, I would be working out with the Notre Dame football team. He asked if I was going to do the same workouts the players were going to. Well . . . no, I responded.

He ribbed me in reply that I wasn't so much working out *with* the Notre Dame football team as I was working out *near* the Notre Dame football team. Spoken like a true older brother.

Nevertheless, I was pretty excited about my first day working out in the Gug. I was there a little before 7 a.m. on a very cold January morning, and the guys were already warmed up and doing various drills. The practice area is split in half:

There's a turf section that is like a mini football field, and then the other side is all weights. There must be thirty bench press stations and a bunch of things that look menacing—and heavy. I found an elliptical machine that was right between the two sections and started it up. After a couple minutes, I took my headphones off since the music in the weight room was pumping loud enough that I couldn't hear what was coming through my own headphones. So I decided to work out to their music and broaden my horizons.

There were songs that I had never heard before, songs that I never wanted to hear again, a few that I recognized, and even a couple that I added to my workout playlist. I can't attest to whether the lyrics of "Purple Lamborghini" by Skrillex (with Rick Ross) or the Jay-Z remix of "Jungle" by X Ambassadors are edifying, but I dig the beats! To be fair, I get to impose my own music preferences on the team with the Christian songs I play before team Mass to set a prayerful or inspirational tone for worship together.

At one point, I looked up from my machine and I saw one of the guys doing a squat with what I thought was a reasonable amount of weight. A thought crossed my mind: "Hey! That doesn't look too bad, I bet I could . . ." and then he *jumped*. He literally squatted down with all of this weight on his shoulders and then he jumped. If I tried that, that weight would have crushed me like an aluminum can!

In this moment, I was reminded of a story that I told to the team in my homily before the Ball State game in 2018. When I was in the seminary, I was complaining to my spiritual director one day about the fact that other guys seemed to have it all together in the seminary—they seemed to all know *exactly* what they wanted to do with their lives and had really great prayer routines, while I was struggling to figure out where God was calling me to serve him and having a hard time staying focused in prayer. It was really frustrating. After I told him this, he got quiet for a second, leaned back, and said, "Oh, so you're breaking the Eleventh Commandment."

I thought, "Hey, man, look. I'm just a seminarian, but I'm preeeeetty sure there are only *ten* commandments." Curious, I asked, "What's the Eleventh Commandment?"

He said, "Thou shall not *compare*."

I thought, "Okay, that's a good one. If there was an Eleventh Commandment, that might be it!"

Comparison creeps into our lives when we find ourselves defining our happiness by someone else's gifts or life or family or whatever. We play the "if only" game: *I'd be a whole lot*

Scan the QR code or visit www.avemariapress.com/pages/pray-like-a-champion-today-resources to listen to Fr. Nate's pre-Mass playlist on Spotify.

happier if only I had his family. If only I just had her talents. If only I looked like that person, if only I were as smart as her, if only I had that person's house or car. If only, if only, if only. This kind of comparison nearly *instantly* robs us of happiness and makes sure that fulfillment is always juuust around the corner.

Comparative desire, by the way, is often the goal of television or social media advertisements. They bombard us with messages to inspire envy: *You need more! You don't look good enough! Your life will be more organized, more productive, more fulfilling, if you just buy X. Then! THEN! You will be happy.* I'm sad to say how often this works on me.

We all break this Eleventh Commandment. It is baked into our lives through media and commerce, so we might think this is no big deal—but it *is* a big deal. In fact, a 2016 University of Pittsburgh study concluded that heavy users of social media are 2.7 times more likely to be *clinically depressed.*

Why? Because their exposure to "highly idealized representations of peers on social media elicits feelings of envy and the distorted belief that others lead happier, more successful lives." As my friend Trish Maher puts it, with social media, we wonder why everyone else's life looks like a highlight reel while our own lives feel like a blooper reel. With comparison, we push away happiness and gratitude for what God has given each of us with a steady stream of "if onlys."

Comparison is not the path to happiness—*gratitude* is. Each of us has been given unique and beautiful gifts, and it's through these gifts that the Lord wants us to live out our vocations and Christian call. When we become fixated on what we *don't* have and what others *do*, we can become paralyzed into inaction and stuck in our thoughts.

How foolish would it be for me to compare my middle-aged priest workout to the workout of a college-aged elite football player? That day on the elliptical, I laughed at myself for making this momentary comparison and breaking the Eleventh Commandment. I got back to my workout, giving thanks to God for what I have, what I am, and asking for the grace to live out the work he has entrusted to me in the day ahead.

PRAY LIKE A CHAMPION

Today, pray for the grace to grow in gratitude for the person God made you to be and for the circumstances of your life that he has placed you in. Then ask God to help you better understand and act on what he is calling you to do at the intersection of these gifts and circumstances.

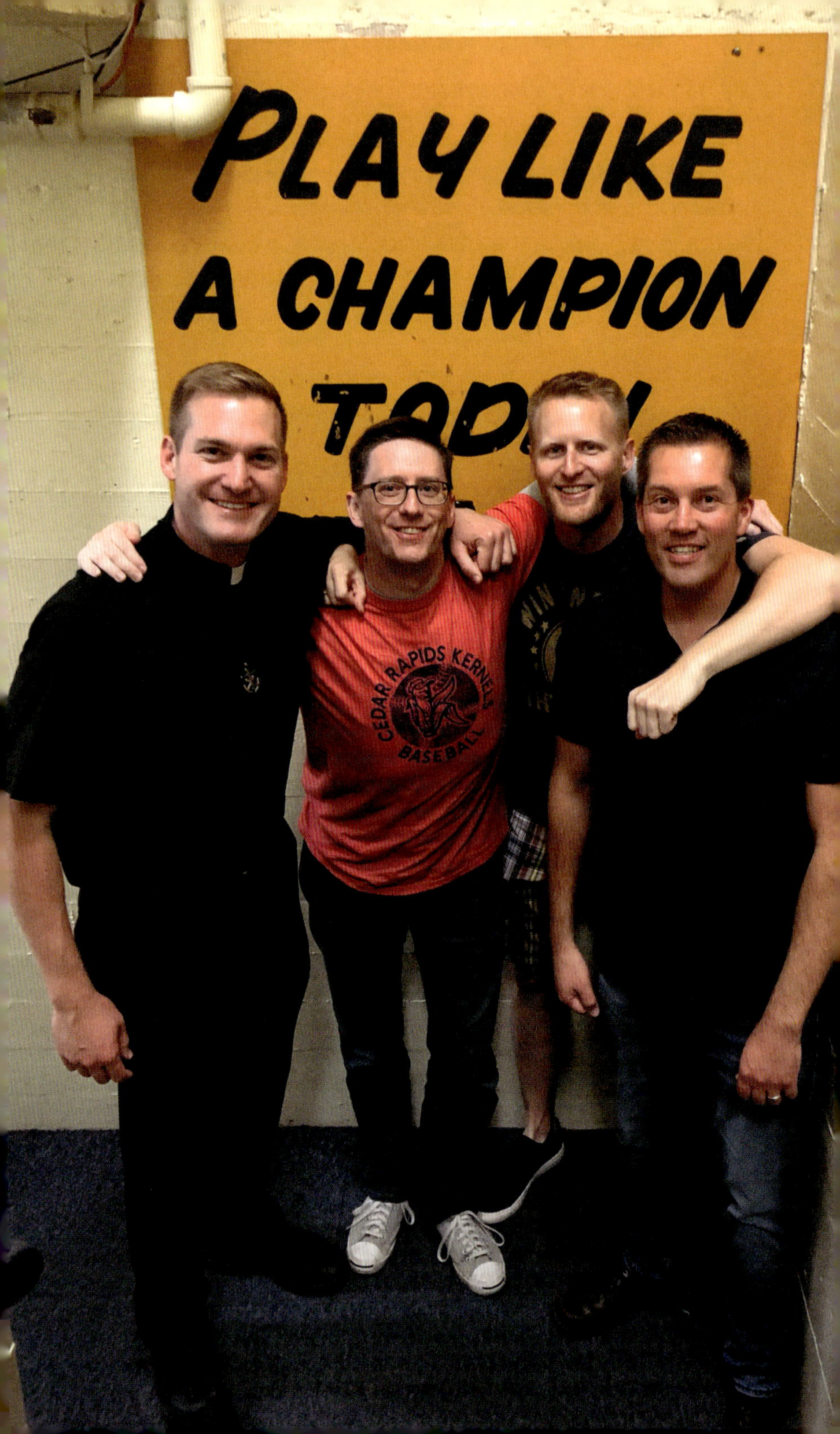
PLAY LIKE
A CHAMPION
CEDAR RAPIDS KERNELS
BASEBALL

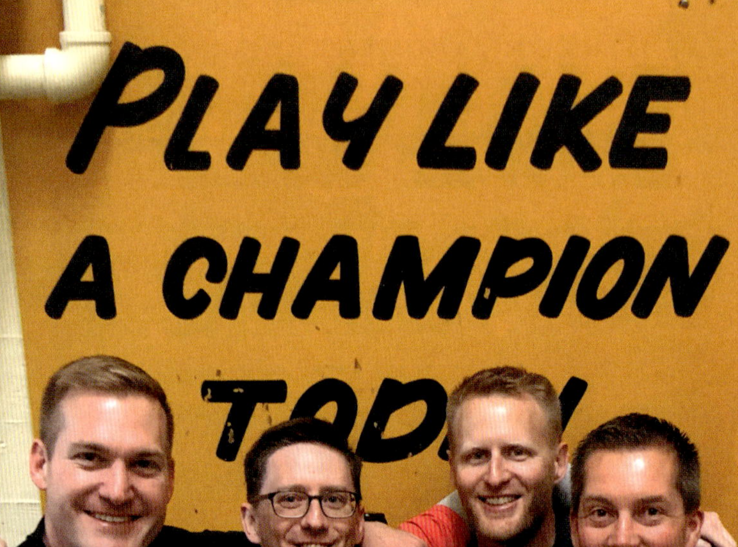

CHAPTER 9

THE GOOD STUFF

I have three buddies from high school who have come to a Notre Dame football game every year for the past twenty-two seasons. We all went to a Catholic, all-boys, military, college-prep high school called Saint Thomas Academy in Mendota Heights, Minnesota. Their names are Bob Lehr, Rob Rogers, and Mark Laliberte. I met these three guys as high school freshmen, and over the years, they have become like brothers to me. I love these guys to death, and I'm constantly amazed at their brilliance, wit, kindness, and loyalty. Our lives, jobs, and vocations take us in different directions, but we always make an effort to get to at least one Notre Dame football game together each year.

There's rarely an agenda for our time together—somehow just hanging out, eating, and going to the game provides ample entertainment. Usually within about thirty minutes of us being together, my face starts to hurt from laughing and smiling so hard. The one exception to not having an agenda was when we made a trip to Chicago to celebrate our fortieth birthdays. We all decided each one of us would get to pick one thing for the group to do—and everybody had to join in for it. This led to an epic weekend where we took on indoor skydiving, an escape room, a show at The Second City comedy club, and a steak dinner where we all had to wear suits. We all would have dressed up anyway, but Bob insisted that we all wear suits. It was amazing.

For Notre Dame games, however, there's usually no agenda other than where we are going to eat. And we don't just gather for home games—they came to the 2021 game where Notre Dame beat Wisconsin at Soldier Field in Chicago; they made the herculean effort to go to the 2023 Shamrock Series game against Navy in Dublin, Ireland; and they all came to the National Championship game in Atlanta in 2025.

They have a tradition of bringing me a thank-you gift for the weekend (against my pleas not to!). One year, they brought me an incredibly rare bottle of bourbon. All of us share an appreciation and enjoyment of bourbon, and as they presented me with this bottle, Rob told me, "Save it for a really special moment. This is the good stuff."

I thanked all of them profusely and proceeded to put it in a place of prominence in my bourbon collection.

And then I paused for a moment. It occurred to me that this *was* a really special moment—what the heck was I waiting for? These guys took vacation days off of work, figured out home responsibilities, and then traveled hours and hours by car to visit me. This was the *one* guaranteed time we were getting together that year. What was I doing? Packing the bottle away for some *other* time? I picked up the bottle, unwrapped the seal, and poured a generous dram for each of us. It was a great moment where all of us were able to recognize and celebrate how much each of us valued our friendship.

I told that story during my homily at the team Mass before the 2022 game against Southern Cal, and I know that it's not great to mention alcohol in a homily to a group of undergraduates (so no need to write me a strongly worded email!). But the point of this story was friendship, brotherhood, and

waking up to the moment. The gospel reading for that Mass was from Luke 21, where Jesus says, "Be vigilant at all times and pray that you have the strength to escape the tribulations that are imminent and to stand before the Son of Man."

This passage is about being awake and alert for the coming of Christ. But this wake-up call doesn't just apply to our readiness for Jesus's Second Coming at the end of time—it is an invitation to be aware of his presence *right here and now*!

For several years, when breaking a huddle, players said three letters: F-T-B! It meant "for the brotherhood," which was a powerful way of grounding their motivation in friendship, fellowship, and the bonds that are forged through intense training and battling together. Friendship and brotherhood in Christ have been a cornerstone of Notre Dame football since the beginning, yet we can lose sight of the importance and beauty of this legacy of faith. When the pressures of big games, media noise, and future implications of wins and losses

become overwhelming, we can all lose sight of the bonds of brotherhood that are truly important in forming a team.

So sometimes we need to wake up to the presence of Jesus among us in the beauty of the everyday friendships right in front of us. This was the challenge I laid before the team in my homily on that day we played Southern Cal, and it was the lesson I had learned from my high school buddies.

One of the most beloved saints in the Christian tradition, St. Francis of Assisi, knew well the value of friendship. The basement crypt of San Francesco Church in Assisi, Italy, where he is buried is one of the most beautiful places I have ever prayed: It simply radiates holiness and peace. It's tempting to simply remain seated or kneeling in the pews there, basking in the serenity and warm glow of a saint whose witness to poverty and a radical embrace of the way of Jesus has inspired centuries of faithful people.

But if you walk around the main altar, you can see that St. Francis isn't the only one buried there. In the four corners around him are the names and burial sites of Leo, Ruffino, Massio, and Angelo. These were the Franciscan brothers who were the great saint's closest friends, who stood by him until the end. None are recognized as saints, yet all were brothers and friends in Christ who supported and encouraged one another in following Christ with profound counter-cultural fidelity. It's not clear if Francis requested this configuration or if perhaps each of them requested to be buried by his side. Quite possibly, their brothers who survived them all knew that it was just the right thing to do to bury these friends near each other so they would be as close in death as they were in life.

No one achieves sainthood alone. And no one achieves greatness alone. Hall of Fame hockey player and six-time

Scan the QR code or visit www.avemariapress.com/pages/pray-like-a-champion-today-resources to watch the Irish lean on a tradition of brotherhood as they prepare for the 2023 season.

Stanley Cup champion Mark Messier titled his memoir *No One Wins Alone*. The truth of this simple statement resounds through the centuries. There's a reason why Jesus sent seventy-two disciples out, two-by-two, to spread his Good News (Luke 10:1). As we try to live out the Christian life, we need to lean on others. All of us need support and friendship here on earth to help us, to challenge us, to journey with us, to encourage us, and sometimes to carry us forward toward our Lord. Our truest friends embody God's love and truth for us, and that's a gift worthy of our gratitude.

We ended up losing to Southern Cal in 2022, 27–38. Michael Mayer's 8 receptions for 98 yards, including 2 touchdowns, couldn't hold back the seemingly unstoppable Trojan quarterback, Caleb Williams, that game. Weeks later, I heard from a friend of mine who is a professor here at Notre Dame. He recounted to me the details of the homily I gave about Mark, Rob, and Bob. I was surprised and asked him how the

heck he knew that story. It turned out that All-American offensive tackle Joe Alt was in his class, which impacted Joe enough that he used that story as an example of appreciating what's right in front of you in one of his papers.

Throughout our lives, true friends are there to pick us up when we fall and to raise a glass with us when we succeed. They help us keep things in perspective and encourage us to live in gratitude for the gifts God has given us. Each year on January 28, the feast day of St. Thomas Aquinas, Mark sends out a picture of all of us together with a quote from the great saint scholar: "There's nothing on earth more to be prized than true friendship."

Forget the loss to Southern Cal. Forget great bourbon. Great and enduring friendships—that's the good stuff.

PRAY LIKE A CHAMPION

Today, pray for your friends. Then reach out to tell them that you are grateful for the ways they keep you going.

CHAPTER 10

PLEASE, GOD, NOT HIS KNEE

You know things are going well for the team if the following people have nothing to do during the game: me and the team doctors. If I can keep my rosary tucked in my pocket and there's no chatter on the doctor's headsets, we have a healthy lead and a healthy team.

The small but elite group of medical professionals on the sidelines of every game are absolutely some of my favorite people. I knew a few of the docs serving the team, including one of our orthopedic surgeons, Dr. Brian Ratigan, from my first assignment as a priest at their parish in South Bend. The whole staff supporting the physical health of the team—from doctors and trainers to nutritionists—bring more than just their expertise to the program. They have big hearts, they believe in this place, and they want to win.

The team docs, especially Dr. Ratigan—who actually played for the Irish—know a ton about football and will often break down a play for me or point something out on a video-board replay that I would have otherwise missed. At times, they also call me into injury situations to pray with parents, to talk to student-athletes who know their season is cut short or ended, or to just offer a close, calming presence when things seem uncertain.

I remember the first time they called me into service in the midst of the 2018 undefeated regular season. Notre Dame was playing Navy in beautiful San Diego. At some point during the first half of the game, Drue Tranquill went down with a leg injury—he was a fifth-year graduate student and team captain, and he was also newly married. Before I even knew what was happening, they whisked him off the field and into the X-ray area. Dr. Ratigan heard all of this on his headset and came over to me to ask if I could say a prayer for Drue—it looked bad, and the replay showed his knees bending in a way that was unnatural and painful to even watch. Dr. Ratigan pointed me toward the tunnel. And as I walked up, I could see an usher standing at the top of the ramp. Before I could say who I was looking for, the usher pointed and said, "He's that way."

I turned the corner to see the football program chief of staff, Beth Rex, standing outside a door with several people. The door was marked with an X-ray warning, and I approached Beth and the two people she was speaking with. As I suspected, the group included Drue's parents, Shannon and Tony. Shannon was speaking on the phone with a measured but clearly nervous intensity, telling Drue's wife what they knew.

I introduced myself to Tony, and he almost involuntarily cried out, "Just not his knee. Please, God, not his knee." Soon after, Shannon got off the phone and I introduced myself to her. Tony said, "We're not Catholic, but we're believers." I smiled tightly and told them that I was the chaplain to all the players, no matter their faith. Then I asked them if they wanted to pray. With a look that was a mix of grief and relief, Shannon said, "Yes, please."

We huddled up and linked hands. We prayed for Drue, his wife, his parents, and all of his family and friends. We prayed for those who were caring for him. We called upon the healing mercy of Jesus and asked that the Lord would send his angels to surround Drue and keep him from harm. And finally, we prayed that fear and uncertainty might be conquered by peace and faith in Jesus Christ, our Redeemer.

The prayer took probably less than a minute, and all the while, I could hear Shannon sniffing as tears flowed and Tony whispering heartfelt affirmations to my prayer. We concluded with an Our Father, and I squeezed their hands with an "Amen" at the end. Just as they thanked me, Beth came walking toward us. "It's not fractured," she said, smiling with relief.

Shannon and Tony hugged each other, and I headed back to the sidelines. I walked toward Dr. Ratigan, but before I could tell him, he already knew that it wasn't a fracture—news traveled through his headset faster than I did. He smiled at me, "Looks like your first miracle, huh?" He clapped me in the shoulder with a big smile.

I chuckled. "What makes you think it's my first?" I replied with a mischievous smile. He got a good laugh out of that, and the game went on.

We were both kidding, of course. To be sure, I believe in miracles, but I don't believe God has given me the gift of performing them in the same way he has given others that gift throughout salvation history (even though some people think this is my role on the team). When the weather is getting bad or we're down several points, I've often had people look to me as if to say, "Can't you do something about this?!" I usually simply reply, "Sorry, I'm in sales, not management."

We pray for miracles all the time, but rarely does God choose to directly intervene in the world that he lovingly created . . . except for when he does. It is hard to make sense of why someone might miraculously walk away from a terrible car accident unscathed while another person is injured for life. It seems as though God should just choose to answer all prayers with miracles or none of them. Anything else can seem random, unfair, and cruel.

During Jesus's earthly ministry, crowds gathered around him to witness his miraculous healings, multiplications, and even raising the dead to life. But he did not always intervene in a miraculous way—think of the moment when he taught in his own hometown of Nazareth and they rejected him. They "took offense" at his teachings and asked in frustration, "Where did this man get all this?" (Matthew 13:56–57). Right after that, the gospel writer notes, "[Jesus] did not work many mighty deeds there because of their lack of faith" (Matthew 13:58). It seems as though *even Jesus* can't perform miracles amid doubt.

By contrast, think of the many times we hear Jesus say in the gospels, "Your faith has healed you"—he said this to the ten lepers, the woman with a hemorrhage, Bartimaeus, and the Syrophoenician woman, to name just a few. Deep faith in Jesus, it seems, is not a guarantee of a miracle; it's the fertile ground that God can work with, if God chooses. Drue and his parents certainly had this depth of faith, and maybe, *just maybe*, something extraordinary *did* happen.

Scan the QR code or visit www.avemariapress.com/pages/pray-like-a-champion-today-resources to watch Drue Tranquill talk about navigating injuries with faith before the 2016 season.

Before the end of the quarter, Drue was standing on the sidelines in a gray boot, telling his relieved teammates that it was likely a "high ankle sprain." If he hadn't been forbidden to do so, I think Drue would have been out there in the second half, playing with a cast on his hand and a boot over his foot.

When we got off the bus from the stadium to return to the

hotel after the game that evening, I saw Drue and his parents standing outside the hotel doors. They shook my hand and thanked me again. Drue told me that he couldn't believe it. "I heard it pop," he said in disbelief. "I know it was broken and now it's not."

I looked at him wide-eyed and said the only thing I could think of in that moment: "Praise God!" His family was brimming with joy and faith in that moment, and as I walked away, I whispered a prayer of thanks to God that I got to witness a miracle.

\\\\\\\\\

PRAY LIKE A CHAMPION

Today, pray for doctors and medical professionals, that they might bring compassion and expertise to ease the suffering of the sick and injured.

\\\\\\\\\

COLLEGE
GAMEDAY
COLLEGE
GAMEDAY
COLLEGE
GAMEDAY

CHAPTER 11

COLLEGE GAMEDAY

My mom plays a game while watching Notre Dame football broadcasts called "spot Fr. Nate." I will sometimes get text messages from my friends, family, students, or colleagues when they catch a glimpse of me on the sidelines when a play runs out of bounds. I always assure them that they didn't mean to put me on TV—it's just that I happened to be standing in front of someone who had a big play. But there was one time in my role as chaplain when they actually *did mean* to show me on TV. It was a moment of complete exhilaration that immediately turned into a waking nightmare.

When ESPN College GameDay came to Notre Dame for the Ohio State game in 2023, a team from Notre Dame Athletics met with ESPN to plan the stories that would be featured in the broadcast segments. Someone floated the idea of including the holy medals that I give our players, even suggesting that I give a holy medal to each of the hosts on the GameDay dais. They sent me an email asking if I would be up for that, and I responded with an enthusiastic "yes!" They asked me if I could send them some information about the tradition of the holy medals, and I responded with a rather lengthy email recounting the history of this tradition that I had recently learned from Fr. Tom Blantz's book.

The next email response from the producers at ESPN said that there was a change of plans. They really liked what I wrote. Could I just say all of that on camera? I stared at the email for a couple seconds to make sure I had read it correctly. *Um. What?!*

I let out a yelp in my office that caused my colleague to come in to check on me. I shared the news, and we collectively freaked out for a little bit. I was going to be on GameDay!

The day of the broadcast arrived, and I showed up at my assigned time. The media folks ushered me into the broadcast area amid the cheering throngs of GameDay fans who were holding signs up and cheering loudly. I got to meet the reporter I was to speak with: GameDay interviewer and Peloton instructor/star Jess Sims! While most know her from her energetic sports reporting or inspirational and encouraging exercise videos on Peloton, Jess is a natural-born teacher and leader. She served in the Teach for America program in Houston right out of college and continued as an elementary school teacher and then assistant principal in New York City, where she created an exercise program for the students in her school.

As a Peloton fan, I can say that her inspirational phrases stick with you long after her workouts. She encourages you to sweat so that you get that "glazed-donut look." She reminds you to do the small things the right way because "how you do anything is how you do everything." And she likes to say, "Purpose in pen, path in pencil," as a way of urging you to stay focused on your goals while not staying locked into precise ways to accomplish them. She often ends her workouts saying, "It's not cliché, it's not corny, it's not a fad. It's called gratitude, and if practiced consistently, it will change your life." I love her fun mix of humor, inspiration,

and energy on her workouts, and I was curious to see what she was like in real life.

She's even better.

Jess was instantly charming and so kind as she went over her notes for my interview. I told her that my last name was Wills, not Will*is* (a mistake she hadn't made, but many people do), and she clarified some of the details of the one-hundred-year history behind the holy medals. I even shared with her a joke I was going to say on-air: When I mentioned that Notre Dame played Army in 1923, I would casually mention that I thought senior GameDay host Lee Corso picked Army to win that game. Big laughs, right?

I never got to make that joke because what happened next was the total nightmare part.

Jess brought me up on a little stage behind the main one and told me we were going on-air soon. They counted it down:

Five. Four. Three. Two. The producer pointed at us, the red light of the boom camera went on, and the crowd went NUTS. In an instant, the crowd noise became deafening, and as exciting as that was, I looked over at Jess in horror to see that she was talking into the microphone—*and I could hear absolutely nothing*. All I saw was her lips moving until she looked over at me. Then, as if in terrifying slow motion, she pointed the microphone at me. I had no idea what she had just said, and the mic was in front of my open mouth. On live TV. On ESPN. In front of eight million viewers. It was a waking nightmare.

I'm sure my pupils were dilated to pinpoints, but I managed to say, "Well, it's great to be with you . . . I have no idea what you just said."

Jess handled it like the total pro she is and covered beautifully, saying that it was understandable as it was so loud. And almost as if she had willed it, the crowd quieted down and I could hear exactly what she said, much to my relief. Thankfully, her kind demeanor and masterful style calmed me down enough to be somewhat coherent through the interview. I was able to talk about the saints on the holy medals as reminders to us that there are many paths to Jesus, and then talked a bit about the medal for this game: St. Mark. I chose it as a shout-out to Coach Marcus Freeman's patron saint because we were playing his alma mater, Ohio State.

I got about a dozen text messages from friends around the nation saying that they saw my segment.

Scan the QR code or visit www.avemariapress.com/pages/pray-like-a-champion-today-resources to watch the ESPN College GameDay segment featuring the holy medals before the 2023 Ohio State game.

Everyone was very kind, and it turns out that my absolute internal terror didn't come across as obviously as I thought it did. As I was exiting the area, I ran into my buddy, Fr. Pete McCormick, CSC, who was set to lead another segment featuring his fantastic DJ skills. I told him about my interview in an adrenaline-fueled barrage of words that was likely incoherent. "Hey," he said with his characteristic enthusiasm, "Way to do your part, baby!"

I walked away with gratitude that I *had* done my part. It was a bit nerve-wracking and clunky, but I was authentic and managed to get across what I had hoped. God can use that, I figured.

That's what Jesus does. The only miracle that's in all four gospels (besides Jesus's resurrection) is the feeding of the five thousand. But there's a detail in John's account that makes it my favorite retelling. When the disciples come to Jesus with an impossible situation—getting enough food to feed the huge crowd that had gathered around him—the apostle Andrew suggests a solution that is completely inadequate, but it's more than anyone else offers. He says, "There is a boy here who has five barley loaves and two fish; but what good are these for so many?" (John 6:9). Jesus takes what the boy had, blesses it and lifts it up in gratitude to the Father, and then distributes as many loaves and fish as the people can eat. The boy in this story did his part, and God used what little he had offered and multiplied it beyond comprehension. This miracle is an encouragement for all of us who find ourselves with offerings to God that seem inadequate, simple, and at times, nerve-wracking and clunky. God can use that.

And he did.

A week later, I got an email out of the blue from someone who had seen the broadcast. It was from a man who had recently lost his brother. He told me that his brother was a brilliant and successful man, but he had some mental-health challenges and looked to alcohol for self-medication. In the last few years of his life, his addiction turned him into a dark and mean husband and father of five children. He spiraled into darkness and eventually died—the family wasn't sure if it was alcohol poisoning or suicide. The man who wrote me the email had fallen away from his faith in the last several years, and the loss of his brother only deepened his sorrow. He wrote,

> I watched GameDay in a hotel room last Saturday while getting ready for my brother's funeral. My wife and I love football and we watch GameDay every week. It might be the one thing we're still religious about! I was surprised to hear, on a football pre-game show, a priest talk about the saints and the wonderful tradition of commemorative saint medals. I was touched by the tradition and impressed by your straightforward, unapologetic expression of faith. But what really touched me was that on my brother Mark's funeral day you selected St. Mark as the saint for the day.
>
> I don't know what I believe about God anymore. I don't know who chooses the football saint or how the decision is made, and I don't really care. I like to think that God reached out to me with a little wink and a smile to help me say goodbye to

> my sweet brother Marko. Thank you for that gift, Father Wills. It meant a lot to me that morning and it still makes me happy when I think about it.

I emailed him back, promising to pray for him and expressing my sympathy for his loss. We had a beautiful back-and-forth exchange of emails, and eventually I asked him if it would be okay if I sent him one of the holy medals of St. Mark. He said yes and asked if I could include one more for Mark's widow.

I was humbled and awestruck at the way God had touched this man's heart. God multiplied my nervous ramblings and made a difference for this man in a difficult moment. That's what God does when, like the boy in John's gospel, we offer what we have to Jesus and allow our Lord to use and multiply it—even if it's small, clunky, and nerve-wracking.

PRAY LIKE A CHAMPION

Today, pray for those who suffer from addictions and compulsive behavior—and for their families—that they might find the strength and vulnerability to reach out for resources to help them thrive.

NCAA

CHAPTER 12

TEAM GLORY

The interlocking ND has to be one of the most recognizable brands in college football and beyond. It doesn't matter where you are in the world—if you're wearing something with an ND monogram on it, you'll likely hear at least one "Go Irish" if you're in a big crowd of people. If you think about what you're really representing when you wear this symbol—or, more to the point, *whom* you're representing—it's an honor and a responsibility to bear the symbol of Our Lady. So it's not surprising that we take branding very seriously at Notre Dame.

A couple years back, I met the guy who is in charge of all branding for Notre Dame Athletics. His name is Tim O'Connor, but everyone just calls him "Oak." Everything from the size of the ND on a workout shirt to the awesome original images of the Four Horsemen that they plastered all over New York City for the Shamrock Series game in 2024 went through Oak's office. Both end zones in Notre Dame Stadium have nine hash marks (for a total of eighteen), each pointing to Our Lady atop the Golden Dome at 42-degree angles as a nod to the year the University was founded, 1842. When the Irish opened the 2023 season in Ireland, we painted huge Celtic knots in the endzones of Aviva Stadium in Dublin that incorporated those same hash marks from Notre Dame Stadium—that was Oak.

Oak told me that when he first took his job, one of the first things he did was make sure all of the shamrocks used

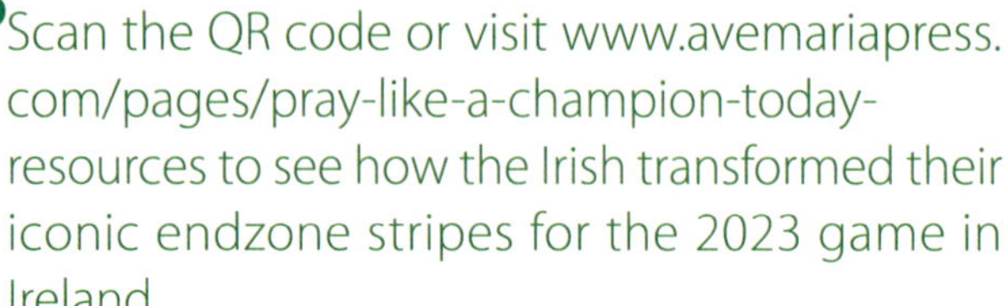

Scan the QR code or visit www.avemariapress.com/pages/pray-like-a-champion-today-resources to see how the Irish transformed their iconic endzone stripes for the 2023 game in Ireland.

by Notre Dame athletics teams had three leaves, not four. This was not a decision prompted only by brand standardization—it was a principled stance. Oak said, "I wanted to make sure they were all three-leaf clovers because that's what St. Patrick used to teach people about the Trinity. *That's* what we stand for at Notre Dame, not some kind of lucky charm."

When he told me that, I smiled and thought, "I like Oak."

Oak's job is to notice when things are off-brand, but in my experience, the sledgehammer of brand enforcement was our former athletic director, Jack Swarbrick—and rightly so, because he's the one who negotiated two ten-year deals for the sports apparel giant Under Armour to outfit Fighting Irish athletics. The night before the Clemson game in 2023, Jack and his wife, Kimberly, hosted a social for all of the coaches and staff. They were, as always, absolutely gracious hosts and a lot of fun. But moments into the evening, Jack looked down at my feet with what started as confusion and then turned into incredulity.

I have a small confession to make: I really like a brand of shoes that are not Under Armour, but they come in all black to match the rest of what I wear as a priest. These particular shoes are subtle in their branding (or so I thought), fit my feet perfectly, and are so comfortable, especially for long stretches of standing. I wear Under Armour for almost everything else, but on this occasion, I got busted.

For the next hour (I'm not exaggerating), Jack busted my chops about this. He had a whole group of people (including myself) roaring with laughter as I dug myself deeper in a hole by the moment.

I tried to argue that these shoes were more comfortable. Jack suggested perhaps I would be more comfortable in the stands instead of on the sidelines. I argued that our women cheerleaders don't wear Under Armour shoes because they don't make cheerleading shoes. He retorted, "Oh, so [this company] makes special clergy shoes?"

The guy went to Stanford Law school. I didn't have a chance. It was like playing capture the flag with Navy Seals. At the end of his good-natured ribbing, Jack said that he hoped readings for the team Mass the next morning were about "repentance!"

As it turned out, they were not. But perhaps even more fittingly, the readings were about one of the most important virtues in living out the Christian life: humility. The gospel reading was from Luke and ended with this beautiful line: "For everyone who exalts himself will be humbled, but the one who humbles himself will be exalted." (14:1, 7–11).

Throughout the gospels, Jesus is constantly encouraging his disciples to embrace humility, serve, and lay down their lives for others. In one of the more cringy moments of the Bible for the disciples, Jesus asks them what they were arguing about as they journeyed to Capernaum (Mark 9:33). No one answered him because they had been debating who among themselves was the greatest. Jesus gathers the twelve apostles and tells them plainly, "If anyone wishes to be first, he shall be the last of all and the servant of all" (Mark 9:35). Humility comes from the word *humus*, meaning "soil" or "dirt." Being humble is about staying grounded, close to the earth, and not getting too high and mighty.

Even though Jack was just kidding around with me, I thought it was a good moment for me to embrace some humility, too, so I decided to "call an audible" on my homily for the next day.

I told the story of what had transpired the night before. The guys got a good chuckle as I recounted my futile arguments and Jack's eviscerating retorts. I told them that this was the reason why I was celebrating Mass without shoes on. The guys looked down at my feet (with Under Armour socks proudly showing!) and chuckled.

I continued by saying that all of us need people to keep us humble, to keep us grounded. It's often our families who do this for us. They remind us who we are and where we have come from. They tell us when it's time to take it down a notch or to step up and do some dishes. I quoted C. S. Lewis's great line: "Humility is not thinking less of yourself, it's thinking of yourself *less*."

The Christian life challenges us to not get caught up in our own individual needs and worries so that we can better orient ourselves toward serving others—so that we can think about our team. Coach Freeman's mantra is that we play for "team glory"—an ideal that is impossible without humility. Staying grounded and humble also helps us to be honest about our gifts and strengths while acknowledging our imperfections and need for Jesus in our lives. Countless self-help books and social media influencers would have us believe that we're perfect *just as we are.* That's not true! We're in need of a savior!

When he was newly elected, Pope Francis famously responded to a reporter's question of "Who is Pope Francis?" with a beautiful line: "I am a sinner whom the Lord has looked upon." We, too, are sinners whom Jesus has looked upon with mercy and has redeemed. The virtue of humility helps us remember who we are, who we are not, and why we need Christ Jesus as our savior.

The game that week was a humbling experience where the Irish lost a heartbreaker to Clemson, 23–31, despite a fourth-quarter fumble recovery by Rylie Mills that almost sparked a comeback. Graciously, no one blamed the loss on my shoes.

Soon after that game, our equipment manager told me that he had something for me. He didn't say whether Jack had tipped him off or if word of my shoeless homily got around. With a big smile, he handed me two pairs of black Under Armour shoes.

PRAY LIKE A CHAMPION

Today, pray for the gift of humility, that you might rightly see your place in the world as God's beloved and grow in freedom to follow his promptings instead of false praise or fear.

CHAPTER 13

ONE LIFE

There are four rules posted in the weight room of the Gug. They're simple, meaningful, and strictly enforced with an immediate consequence: pushups. They were created by former Notre Dame head of strength and conditioning, Matt Balis—you might remember him as having the loudest, gravely, quintessentially strength-coach voice you have ever heard. I first noticed the sign listing the rules when I was practicing a homily before a Mass with the team in the auditorium of the Gug. I had written notes on my phone and wanted to find a quiet place to read over them before Mass, so I went into the weight room and sat down on one of those big boxes that guys jump on—for workouts. And as I looked up from the notes on my phone, I saw a big sign that listed these rules of the weight room: No sitting. No yawning. No cell phones. Notre Dame gear only (which is all branded with Under Armour).

I looked at this sign and then at myself. I wasn't wearing Under Armour shoes, and I was sitting down, looking at my cell phone, and likely yawning. If Coach Balis saw all that, I would have been doing pushups all day!

I love these rules because they're such practical manifestations of ideals that are hard to instill in others: a sense of urgency and a sense of identity.

Those first two rules—no sitting and no yawning—accomplish a similar goal: creating a culture of intensity and intentionality. Coach Freeman likes to say, "One play, one life!" to remind us that we only get one shot at living well. God has given each of us one chance to live out our life here on earth, and it's up to us to make it count. There's no sitting or yawning because even if it's 6:30 a.m., you gotta move with purpose and eagerness. There's no time to waste. Get to work!

Scan the QR code or visit www.avemariapress.com/pages/pray-like-a-champion-today-resources to watch Coach Freeman inspire the team with his "One Life" message during the 2022 season.

This sense of urgency translates to other parts of life as well. I've had the privilege of getting to know Notre Dame football alum Pat Eilers over the years, and it's clear that he is a person who has translated a sense of urgency that he developed playing football into a successful business career. After playing on the 1988 national championship team, Pat graduated from Notre Dame with a degree in biology in 1989—and then graduated with a second degree in mechanical engineering in 1990. He played in the NFL for six years, and after retiring, he went back to school to earn a master's degree in business administration from Northwestern. He took all that knowledge and hustle and founded an investment firm. It's never surprising to me when former players are doing well in their careers. They're not afraid to work hard, lock in, and make the most of the one life that God has given them.

This sense of urgency isn't just applicable to successful careers; it also pertains to Jesus's invitation to follow him. The first words Jesus speaks in the Gospel of Mark are ones of urgency: "This is the time of fulfillment. The kingdom of

God is at hand. Repent, and believe in the gospel" (1:15). When Jesus calls Peter and Andrew as they are fishing, they respond immediately: "At once they left their nets and followed him" (Matthew 4:20). They saw someone so compelling that they dropped what they were doing and followed him *at once*. Their urgency is a beautiful example to us who seek faith—they challenge us to cut through the excuses we make to ourselves about following Jesus.

That's where the next weight room rule comes in: no cell phones. As helpful as technology is, we carry in our pockets the most powerful temptations to distraction in human history. Social media, games, news, email, and videos are all available to us 24/7 and want one simple thing from us: our attention. This is the goal of every commercial, marketing ploy, or viral video: to get and keep our eyes focused on their product or service.

In his lively book *The Anthropocene Reviewed*, John Green calls out the widespread falsehood that we think we can multitask with technology. He says that a tiny fraction of the general population can actually do this, and most of them end up being fighter pilots. He tells it straight: You're not a fighter pilot.

In *The Screwtape Letters*, C. S. Lewis writes about the power of distraction. In this book, he imagines a senior demon writing to his junior demon nephew to give him advice on how to tempt a young Christian away from the faith. This senior demon refers to God as "the Enemy" and encourages the junior demon to lead his charge into distraction:

> The Christians describe the Enemy as one "without whom Nothing is strong." And Nothing is very strong: strong enough to steal away a man's best years not in sweet sins but in a dreary flickering of the mind over it knows not what and knows not why, in the gratification of curiosities so feeble that the man is only half aware of them, in drumming of fingers and kicking of heels, in whistling tunes that he does not like, or in the long, dim labyrinth of reveries that have not even lust or ambition to give them a relish, but which, once chance association has started them, the creature is too weak and fuddled to shake off.

I'm not saying that cell phones lead us down the road to perdition, but I *do* think there's wisdom in being attentive to what we're doing and being aware of what or who is consuming our time and attention. When you lift, *lift*. When you pray, *pray*. Pay attention, lock in, and reject the distractions that keep you from being fully alive in Christ. We only get one life.

Okay, the final weight room rule: Notre Dame gear only. While this rule is a pragmatic one that focuses on a consistency of branding, I think there's something beautiful about bringing intentionality to what student-athletes are wearing so they simply focus on representing Notre Dame. There are no advertisements for other schools or brands allowed in the weight room. All of us bear the name of Mary—Notre Dame, our mother—on our clothing. I'm hopeful that this not only forges a sense of pride in the University for these student-athletes, but also charges them to act, live, and serve in a way that makes our moms here on earth proud and our heavenly mother smile.

Notre Dame means "Our Lady" in French, and that first word is really important. The fact that we claim Mary as *our* mother means we're taking the gift of Jesus on the Cross seriously—he told the beloved disciple, "Behold, your mother" (John 19:27) and gave Mary as a mother to us all. She's our intercessor with her son, Jesus, and an inspiration for us as we seek to imitate the way that she said yes when God asked her to carry his Son. We, too, are invited to carry Jesus with us and to reveal his presence through our lives.

Notre Dame isn't just written on our shirts—her name is written on our hearts. For me, this rule isn't just about consistency of branding and uniformity; it's about identity. Wearing the name of Our Lady on our shirts reminds us of who we are, of the one we're called to imitate, and of the tradition that we all step into at this University.

Coach Balis left our team a couple years ago, but his four rules are still up there on the wall of the weight room. Maybe they'll be removed, changed, or modified someday, but for now, I think they're great reminders that whether we're lifting weights or living out the Gospel, we do it with an intentionality, a sense of urgency, and knowing our identity as a beloved child of Notre Dame, our mother.

PRAY LIKE A CHAMPION

Today, pray for your mother—whether she's still alive or in heaven—and ask her to pray for you.

CHAPTER 14

THE ULTIMATE CHAMPION

My role as chaplain sometimes extends beyond the sidelines. In mid-December 2024, I was asked to represent the University at the funeral of a man of great faith who coached at Notre Dame from 1981 to 1985, Gerry Faust. I joined a rather esteemed delegation from the University's Athletics and Alumni departments. Of that entire group, I think I was the only person who had never actually met Coach Faust in person. Several people in the Athletics Department knew him through his ongoing close connection to Notre Dame. Fr. Paul Kollman, CSC, was attending the funeral with us and actually had Coach Faust as a gym teacher at the high school in Cincinnati, Archbishop Moeller High School, where he became a legendary football coach.

I knew very little about Coach Faust's life—only what I had heard in Notre Dame football lore. If you're a big Notre Dame football fan, you already know that in 1981, when Dan Devine retired, Notre Dame hired Faust based on his wildly successful high school football career. Many referred to his promotion from Moeller head coach right to Notre Dame head coach as "the Bold Experiment," given his lack of experience coaching at the collegiate level. But for Coach Faust, who was a devout Catholic, being the head coach at Notre Dame was a dream come true.

Scan the QR code or visit www.avemariapress.com/pages/pray-like-a-champion-today-resources to watch highlights from Coach Faust's first win, a 1981 home victory over LSU.

The experiment didn't quite work out, and Faust ended his career after five seasons at Notre Dame with a record of 30 wins, 26 losses, and 1 tie. He never lost his love for Notre Dame, though, and often came back to the campus he loved so much and only grew in his devotion to Our Lady, Mary, its namesake. He never lost his sense of perspective and humor about his career, either. While we were traveling to the funeral, Coach Kevin Corrigan, who had just led Notre Dame's lacrosse team to back-to-back national titles, told the story about a call he got from Coach Faust early in his career. He asked Coach Corrigan if he wanted some advice. Corrigan eagerly assented. Faust paused a beat and said, "Don't go 30-and-26-and-1 like I did!"

The funeral was held at St. Hillary Parish in a suburb of Akron, Ohio, where Gerry and his wife, Marlene, had retired. When we arrived, the church was absolutely packed with family, friends, parishioners, and other priests. A dozen or so students wearing Moeller letter jackets stood like sentinels in the main aisle of the church before the ceremony began.

The opening song was a Catholic classic, "Here I Am, Lord," and I joined the small army of concelebrating priests in the procession through the church. I slid into the third row of pews next to Fr. Paul and sat after the opening rites and prayer. Flipping through the funeral program, I saw a familiar name. There were two names listed as eulogists: One I didn't recognize, and another listed was John Boehner. "Huh!" I thought—it was spelled the same way as the former Speaker of the House. I turned my program to Fr. Paul and pointed to the name. He nodded and asked, “Did you see him when we processed in?” I was confused. How would I know what some random guy looked like? *Unless* (it finally clicked) it actually *was* former Speaker John Boehner. Fr. Paul must have seen the look on my face and kept his response simple, not wanting to be disruptive during the funeral. He said simply, “Moeller grad.”

Turns out, John Boehner played linebacker under Coach Faust when he attended Archbishop Moeller High School in the mid-1960s. Toward the end of a beautiful and heartfelt Mass (seriously, afterward the ND crew were all blown away at the way *everyone* in that church sang!), it came time for the eulogies. The first eulogy and the name that I didn’t recognize turned out to be one of Gerry’s teenage granddaughters, who was very close to her grandfather and gave a lovely eulogy. Speaker Boehner was up next. No matter what your political point of view might be, I don’t think *anyone* could deny that it was an absolutely wonderful tribute to Coach Faust. In it, he quoted an article that was once written about Coach Faust, talking about his career as a motivational speaker later in life:

> Coach Faust faced failure in his own life, and it couldn’t keep him down. “People listen to me because I’m not all about success,” Coach Faust once told *Sports Illustrated*. “They’ll listen to someone who failed because most people fail at something in life.”

This vulnerability and honesty absolutely blew me away. Coach Faust recognized that his relatability as a person and credibility as a speaker was grounded in his failures, not his successes.

Success is an elusive goal. It always stays just out of our reach, and rarely do its pursuers claim that they’ve actually achieved and held it. What is *success* anyway? Is it a measure of wealth, power, pleasure, happiness, or control? Does it mean simply achieving your goals? For a coach, it’s often a number—their win/loss/tie

record that Gerry Faust was able to joke about. But for us living the Christian life, it's a lot more complicated than that.

St. Teresa of Calcutta famously confronted the world's notion of success head-on when she said, "God did not call me to be successful. He called me to be faithful." This bold rejection of success as a goal of the Christian life sounds countercultural at best, dismissive at worst. But there's true and deep wisdom in that statement.

In Matthew's gospel, Jesus tells his disciples, for the first time, that he is going to have to go to Jerusalem, suffer, and die (16:21–23). None of this sounds like a success, and Peter is so upset that he pulls Jesus aside to "rebuke him." Jesus comes back at him with what must have felt pretty harsh in the moment: "Get behind me, Satan! You are an obstacle to me. You are thinking not as God does, but as human beings do."

Jesus's mission was not about success; it was about laying down his life for us. Jesus turns to all of his disciples and explains, "Whoever wishes to come after me must deny himself, take up his cross, and follow me. For whoever wishes to save his life will lose it, but whoever loses his life for my sake will find it" (Matthew 16:24–25).

This is the Christian life that St. Teresa of Calcutta pointed to. Not success, but faith. Not safety, but sacrifice. Not *having it all*, but *giving it all* in the imitation of the one who didn't hesitate to give his life for all of us.

We all have failed and can stand in admiration of Coach Faust's deep faith that would not let frustration or regret touch his indomitable spirit. He allowed nothing else but his faith in Jesus Christ to define him, and in the end, this is how I will remember him. Speaker Boehner said it best that day:

> Maybe Coach Faust didn't have the run at Notre Dame he always dreamed about. But he never wavered in his love for Notre Dame and what it stood for, and he achieved something far more profound. His life was a towering cathedral to the glory of God—like Notre Dame itself. He lived to the final minute with absolute commitment to his faith and the people he loved. He made everyone he coached, everyone he knew, better, helping them find their own path to heaven, to a chance for eternal life with our Creator.
>
> That kind of faithfulness is the ultimate victory. And Gerry Faust was the ultimate champion.

PRAY LIKE A CHAMPION

Today, pray for those who have gone before us in the Notre Dame family of faith, that God might welcome them into the joy of heaven.

CHAPTER 15

OUR LADY, QUEEN OF VICTORY

Since I started posting on Instagram about the holy medals that I distribute to players and coaches, people often ask why I chose a particular saint for a given game. Coach Freeman's wife, Joanna, absolutely *loves* the holy medal tradition, and will ask me this question every game without fail. I've already described the five-year rotation of the medals, and based on my supplier's availability, I have been able to add or retire some. So putting together the lineup for a season is a kind of puzzle.

At the beginning of the season, I will sit down with three things: the list of saints on that year's rotation, our football schedule, and a liturgical calendar. Fr. Mark had a column in his clever spreadsheet for the saint's feast day and often tried to line these up. He also had the great idea to have one medal of the Blessed Virgin Mary each season. Those medals depict Mary under one of her many titles or apparitions throughout the world, and I will usually schedule that medal for what might be a big game for the upcoming season.

Over the years, I've tried to change things up a bit by adding in a mix of saints who represent different regions of the world, time periods, religious communities, ages, races, as well as saints who are men or women . . . or neither (in the case of angels!). The good folks at Notre Dame football have been very supportive, even when I had to pay more to a new supplier to get medals of St. Josephine Bakhita, a woman from Sudan who died in 1947, for our New Year's Day Fiesta Bowl in 2022, for example.

Beyond choosing saints because we might play a game near their feast day, I sometimes have room to be a little creative. My favorite example of this was when Notre Dame played Navy in November 2022 at M&T Bank Stadium, the home field of the Baltimore Ravens. For that game, I chose one of the medals that might not be the most readily apparent choice, but it was already listed in the rotation for that year: Our Lady of the Rosary—or as it appeared on the medal, "Queen of the Most Holy Rosary."

Our Lady of the Rosary has a very important naval connection and a fascinating history. In 1571, an epic battle at sea took place that would shape Western civilization. The Ottoman Empire had been expanding fairly aggressively across the Mediterranean and threatened the maritime trading routes of European countries. Pope Pius V formed a coalition of Christian states to unify against the powerful Ottoman navy. This alliance between places who had historically been rivals—Spain, Venice, Malta, Genoa, the Papal States, and others—formed what they called the "Holy League" (which definitely sounds like an idea for a Christian superhero movie!).

The Ottoman fleet had not lost a significant battle in more than a century, yet the combined navy of the Holy League engaged them in the historic Battle of Lepanto off the western coast of Greece. In preparation for this battle, the faithful across those different allied lands were asked to pray, day and night, for the protection of Mary, Our Lady of the Rosary.

The Holy League was victorious and signaled to the Ottoman Empire that the collective action of European resistance could successfully challenge their expansion.

There is a depiction of the Battle of Lepanto in the stained-glass windows of one of the side chapels of the Basilica of the Sacred Heart at Notre Dame. Before the Navy game in 2022, I went into the basilica to take pictures of these windows for my Instagram post. I ran into the sacristan, John Zack, and asked if he knew anything about this window. He told me that a book had just been written about the stained-glass windows in the basilica, and he let me borrow a copy of Nancy Cavadini and Cecilia Cunningham's amazing book, *Stories in Light*. In it, I read a story about these windows that I had never known before, but that forever changed the way I see them.

The book recounts a story about the founder of the University of Notre Dame, Fr. Edward Sorin, CSC, who made nearly fifty voyages across the Atlantic during his lifetime. On one of his trips in 1875, Fr. Sorin left from a New York harbor on a steamship across the Atlantic. Eight days into his journey, his ship became disabled and drifted off course. He and his shipmates were lost at sea with little hope of rescue. Sorin knew of the story of Our Lady of the Rosary and turned to her, leading his shipmates in daily prayers for her intercession. Against all odds, they were found after fifteen days adrift.

Sorin credited their miraculous rescue to Mary's intercession and changed the plans of his campus church to include one side chapel dedicated to Our Lady of the Rosary under her original name, Our Lady of Victory. I had never known that this was called the "Victory Chapel" in the Basilica of the Sacred Heart—and it is adjacent to the space where we celebrate Mass before every home game.

Scan the QR code or visit www.avemariapress.com/pages/pray-like-a-champion-today-resources to view Fr. Nate's Instagram post showing the Our Lady of the Rosary holy medal, an amazing catch by Braden Lenzy, and the stained-glass windows that depict the Battle of Lepanto in the Basilica of the Sacred Heart.

That title for Mary as Our Lady of Victory is close to the hearts of our players and coaches. Immediately before we take the field, the last thing our team does is to take a knee, pray the Our Father, and invoke her intercession as I shout, "Our Lady, Queen of Victory!"—and they respond in a booming chorus, "PRAY FOR US!"

When I told this story about the history behind our connection to Our Lady, Queen of Victory, I saw Assistant Athletic Director Ron Powlus's mouth fall open in surprise. During pregame warm-ups, Ron brought our athletic director, Jack Swarbrick, over to me and said, "Tell him the story." Connecting a naval battle to Notre Dame's history and the intercession we call upon before every game makes for a great story, and it reminds us that we are part of something much bigger than ourselves.

As it turned out, we definitely needed her intercession during that game against Navy. The Irish came out strong in the first half with 35 points, including one of the most spectacular catches I have ever seen by Braden Lenzy—he literally caught the ball behind the back of his defender and somehow muscled it into his possession to score a touchdown. But despite Drew Pyne's four touchdown passes, including one to Jayden Thomas who racked up 80 receiving yards, the Irish offense cooled down in the second half and Navy stormed back.

I keep a rosary in my pocket every game, and when games like this one get close, I do what Notre Dame fans at home throughout the nation and world do, too—I reach for it and start praying. I don't pretend to think that my individual prayers will change the course of the game one way or the other, but I figure it can't hurt.

After all, legendary Notre Dame coach Lou Holtz likes to tell the story of the luncheon before the 1988 game against Miami. As he tells it, before the chaplain for the University of Miami, who was a Catholic priest, gave the invocation at lunch, he said, "God doesn't care who wins this game" and blessed the food. Lou then got up and said, "I agree with you. God does not care who wins this game. But I want to promise you, his mother does."

Scan the QR code or visit www.avemariapress.com/pages/pray-like-a-champion-today-resources to watch a speech from former head coach Lou Holtz at a pep rally before the 2013 Southern Cal game.

Does our prayer have the power to affect things like the outcome of a game or the health of a sick family member? I can assure you this, God doesn't always answer my prayers the way I want, otherwise we would have been national champions every year since I started with the team! Yet throughout his ministry, Jesus invited people to lift up their prayers to our loving God. From the Lord's Prayer to parables like the persistent widow (Luke 18:1–8) or the friend at midnight (Luke 11:5–13), Jesus is often telling his disciples to remain faithful in prayer. He himself often withdrew from the crowds to pray.

Even when he faced arrest, trial, and execution, Jesus stepped away to spend time praying in the Garden of Gethsemane and asked the Father to let this cup of suffering pass him by. In that prayer, Jesus said something significant: "Yet, not as I will, but as you will" (Matthew 26:39). This acceptance echoes how he teaches his disciples to pray in the Lord's Prayer: "*Thy* will be done." As we lift up our prayers to God, we are invited to let go of the outcomes, trusting that the Lord who has taken care of us will continue to show his love and compassion. To be sure, I often pray "thy will be done" when I really mean "*my* will be done" and can become frustrated with God when things don't go the way I want them to. In looking back over my life, however, I can see God at work in the situations I prayed about—just in surprising and unexpected ways.

While we would gladly avoid disappointments, pain, and loss, that's simply not the human condition. We were created for more—for a life beyond this one—and in lifting up our prayers, we're communicating our joys and woes to our compassionate God. Like a parent who doesn't always grant their child's desires, he loves us enough to sometimes deny even our most fervent requests because he has something even better in mind for us.

We don't always get what we want, but if we keep coming back to God in prayer, we receive what we need to face the challenges ahead. Prayer is not without effect, but perhaps it doesn't always have the precise effect we are looking for. Søren Kierkegaard once said, "Prayer does not change God, but it changes him who prays."

Still, sometimes it works. We beat Navy that day, 35–32.

PRAY LIKE A CHAMPION

Today, pray for first responders and for people who serve in our armed forces—as well as their families—that God might keep them safe from harm.

EXIT

CHAPTER 16

O HOLY NIGHT

There aren't a lot of holiday songs that talk about the idyllic Christmas celebration taking place in a hotel meeting room. Okay, there are none. But that's usually what happens for the team around Christmas. Depending on the bowl schedule (and thanks be to God, we've always been invited to a bowl since I've been with the team!), we usually leave campus right around Christmas to get to our destination and end up spending Christmas Day in a hotel.

Christmas Mass with the team is always a touching experience. Unlike our normal team Masses, which are attended by only student-athletes and coaches, families and kids join us for this joyful celebration. On a couple of occasions, we've organized some music, and everybody joins in familiar Christmas carols. Even in a hotel ballroom, it can be surprisingly prayerful.

The exception, of course, was our COVID year, 2020. For Christmas Mass that year, we didn't leave for our bowl game until *after* Christmas, so we celebrated Mass on campus. We set up an altar in the IAC and even put a Christmas message on the big screen. The staff did their best to make it feel festive—in the corner of the Indoor, they piled up colorfully wrapped Christmas presents for the players, and families dressed up in their Christmas best. But there was no denying the less-than-ideal nature of this celebration. Everyone was masked, and chairs were set up at least six feet apart. Chairs covered much of the 100-yard field in the IAC, and as a result, the responses from the congregation were muted at best. I tried to set the tone, making the Sign of the Cross and energetically proclaiming, "The Lord be with you!"

What I got back was a muffled "Mmm wiiii mmmm spiriiiii." As we did through the whole pandemic, we did our best and prayed with and for a broken world. We couldn't sing our traditional, familiar, and comforting Christmas songs, but I had prepared a little surprise for the guys. A couple weeks before our Mass, I reached out to a friend of mine who was completing his PhD in sacred music at Notre Dame. I can guarantee that you've rarely heard someone sing as beautifully as Emorja Roberson. I asked him if he would be willing to record a Christmas song or two that we might play

during Mass. He asked which songs I wanted him to play, and I responded by saying, "It's totally up to you, but I really like 'O Holy Night.' I also like 'O Come All Ye Faithful,' but those are two very different vibes. Do whatever you like!"

A couple days later, he came back to me with a simple video of him sitting at the piano and singing the most heartfelt, warm, and perfect mashup of those two songs. Right after he hits the high note, singing, "Oh niiiight, diviiiiiine," he makes this beautiful and effortless run down a series of chords that somehow leads right into "O Come All Ye Faithful."

The first time I opened it on my computer, I was astounded and thrilled. I had vaguely asked for either, and he had done *both*. I couldn't wait to play it at our Christmas Mass. Then I saw

that he had sent a second video. It's a song I had never heard before, called "Jesus, the Light of the World." Here are the lyrics:

> Walk in the light,
> Beautiful light.
> Come where the dewdrops of mercy shine bright.
> Shine all around us by day and by night.
> Jesus, the light of the world.

Just when I didn't think I could be more moved or astounded, somehow in the midst of that song—as if spiking the metaphorical ball in the endzone—he wove in melodies from "Hark! The Herald Angels Sing." I know something so luminous was bound to hit me a bit harder during all the uncertainty and loneliness of the pandemic, but I stand by my initial reaction. It's beautiful and masterful.

And more than that, it was simply perfect for Christmas. The first Christmas was, to put it mildly, less than ideal as

Scan the QR code or visit www.avemariapress.com/pages/pray-like-a-champion-today-resources to watch Emorja Roberson sing "Jesus, the Light of the World."

well: Joseph and Mary had traveled far from their home and families for the census in Bethlehem. On top of it all, Luke's gospel tells us that Mary had to lay her baby in an animal's feed trough because there was no room at the inn. Luke goes on to describe how shepherds came to worship the child; Matthew recounts wise men from the East paying homage to Jesus. And then Joseph has a dream that they need to flee to Egypt so Herod doesn't kill their baby.

To put it mildly, all of this was less than ideal. Yet it's into this messiness that the Messiah chooses to enter. Jesus, the light of the world, is born into the darkness and comes to transform despair into hope, sadness into joy, and loneliness into a deep and abiding sense of his love for us all.

We played these two songs from Emorja over the sound system at the IAC, and through masks and social distancing, it was tough to gauge the reaction of the players and coaches to these songs. But I can speak for myself: Tears of joy streamed down my face and onto my mask. This music, like Jesus at Christmas, had entered into the messiness and transformed it into a holy night, a night divine.

PRAY LIKE A CHAMPION

Today, pray for those who struggle with depression and despair, that God's light might break upon them and lead them to peace and joy.

MILLS
99
IRISH
CROSS III
PLAY LIKE
A CHAMPION
TODAY
PENN STATE

CHAPTER 17

GOD'S TIME

Two hours before the 2025 Orange Bowl, team captain Rylie Mills propped himself up on a high table in the training area of the Miami Dolphins' locker room. He set his crutches off to the side and got as comfortable as possible for someone who had just had leg surgery the week before. He was wearing the team's white jersey with the Orange Bowl patch over a long-sleeved shirt and was all smiles. Perhaps more so than the crutches, this was a sure sign that he wasn't playing—Rylie never wears sleeves. Even in the biting cold of the first game of the College Football Playoff against Indiana weeks before, he wouldn't have dreamed of allowing himself that comfort. Early in the second half of that game, Rylie sacked quarterback Kurtis Rourke and sustained an injury that meant the end of his season playing for the Irish.

He was home recovering from surgery when the Irish defeated Georgia in the next round of the playoff at the Sugar Bowl. Amid all the jubilation of the locker room after the game, one of his teammates FaceTimed Rylie, and the guys let out an even louder cheer as his face appeared on the phone bouncing up and down to the celebratory music.

Because he was still recovering from surgery, Rylie didn't travel with the team to the Orange Bowl—his doctor ordered him not to fly and to keep his foot elevated. So Rylie decided to get creative. He told me that he rented

an RV that week and his uncle kindly drove him from South Bend to Florida so that he could keep his leg elevated during the whole journey. It was a long drive and a herculean effort, but he wanted to attend the game with his brothers.

We had a great conversation in that Dolphins' training room before the game. He's naturally curious and smart—a guy who is easy to talk to about a variety of topics. In November before the Southern Cal game, I remember sitting down in the team meal room at the hotel in LA and talking to him and Jack Kiser for about forty-five minutes as we gave our hot takes on recent movies, including the overuse of the multiverse as a plot vehicle and a review of *Gladiator II*, which they had just seen. On the other end of the spectrum, I recall standing with him on the sideline when he was done playing in the spring Blue/Gold game and having an extended conversation about exorcisms. Like I said, he's a thoughtful guy.

As he tried to get comfortable on the table, Rylie snapped his fingers and pointed at me to get my attention and said, "I wanted to tell you something!" He told me that he had been thinking a lot about a story I shared in a homily during the 2023 season, which was about God's timing and my brother, Nick.

My older brother Nick is definitely the athlete in our family. He came to Notre Dame the year before I did and joined the men's basketball team as a walk-on his freshman year. He eventually earned a scholarship, playing on John MacLeod's team from 1994 to 1998. Nick has always been one of those guys who is naturally coordinated and graceful—clearly a recessive gene in my family that skipped me!

Along with his athleticism, Nick is driven in a way that I have always admired. He's competitive with others and with himself, and he is always trying to get better (even when he's already really good!). When he was a kid, he got it in his head that he wanted to go to Notre Dame. Throughout high school when he became a star basketball player, he updated that dream—he wanted to play basketball at Notre Dame. His desire to come to Notre Dame was a bit out of nowhere, and to this day he can't really tell you how it came about. My theory is that it was the combination of Notre Dame winning the 1988 national championship in football during our formative years as kids and the release of *Rudy* during the fall of his senior year. It was the perfect storm.

In high school, Nick was an A-student and an all-state basketball player, but we were also first-generation college students and didn't have an alumni connection or any other "in" to a place like Notre Dame. Nick was undeterred. In his relentless pursuit of his dream, he asked a man who

had graduated from Notre Dame, J. Peter Ritten, to write him a letter of recommendation. The exceptionally kind Ritten happily agreed. That spring, Nick was accepted into the class of 1994, and that fall, he made it as a walk-on for the basketball team.

Nick came into his freshman year as a pre-med major and established a new dream to become a doctor. His randomly selected roommate in Fisher Hall, Aaron Ferrell, introduced Nick to his dad, Dr. Craig Ferrell, who was a kind, athletic, generous, and excellent orthopedic surgeon. Now Nick knew what kind of doctor he wanted to be too.

With graduation on the horizon and a clear vision of becoming an orthopedic surgeon, Nick applied to med school his senior year.

He didn't get in.

They put him on a wait-list, but he never got the call for acceptance that fall. He moved back into my parents' house and became the long-term substitute teacher at our high school. I remember coming home for Notre Dame's fall break that year and dropping my suitcase in the room that we shared growing up. There was a single letter pinned to the corkboard on the wall: his rejection letter from the medical school he applied to. I remember thinking that if I had received that rejection letter, I would have thrown it out or maybe even burned it. But he hung it up and looked at it *every morning* as he did his job as a sub and studied to take the MCAT again.

The letter said, "No." Nick heard, "Not yet."

St. Monica is the patron saint of patience because she waited and prayed for years until her son, St. Augustine, turned his life around. But I often think of St. Paul as the unofficial patron saint of patience. He endured imprisonment, physical beatings, shipwrecks, and setbacks of every kind as he preached the Gospel to all who would listen—and many who would not. He saw these challenges in the same way that Nick might: as opportunities to grow in faith and in virtue. In his letter to the Romans, St. Paul writes, "We even boast of our afflictions, knowing that affliction produces endurance, and endurance, proven character, and proven character, hope, and hope does not disappoint, because the love of God has been poured out into our hearts through the holy Spirit that has been given to us" (Romans 5:3–5).

That progression from affliction to endurance to proven character to hope in God beautifully reflects the way that St. Paul trusted that everything works toward our good if we can trust in God and his timing. Though it's hard to see when we face rejection, injury, or disappointment in our lives, St. Paul invites us to persevere, to place our trust in Jesus, to believe in God's faithfulness and goodness.

That spring, Nick received a letter of acceptance to the University of Minnesota Medical School as one of their "preferred candidates." Over the next several years, he excelled in his studies, earned a fellowship, and is now an accomplished orthopedic spine surgeon.

This was the story that Rylie was referring to as he considered his injury and future. He said that Nick's story brought him a lot of comfort in being patient with his injury and trusting that his recovery and future would happen on God's time, not his own. After our chat, Rylie hopped out to the field on his crutches, and we continued chatting a bit during warm-ups. He cheered the Irish to victory over Penn State, 27–24.

Like Nick and Riley, we are called to reframe our setbacks into opportunities and to trust more deeply in the Lord's power to bring good out of any situation. Our timing isn't

Scan the QR code or visit www.avemariapress.com/pages/pray-like-a-champion-today-resources to watch behind-the-scenes highlights from the 2025 playoff victory over Penn State.

always the same as God's timing. But make no mistake: If we persevere in faith, even our afflictions can draw us more closely to Jesus.

PRAY LIKE A CHAMPION

Today, pray for the gift of patience and perseverance, that God might help you meet difficulty with an open heart and endure suffering without resentment, trusting in his faithfulness.

Notre Dame
Irish

CHAPTER 18

WRITING HISTORY

When you think of a person throughout history who best represents Notre Dame, who comes to mind first? Perhaps it's the French founder of the University with a love of the United States and the heart of an entrepreneur, Fr. Edward Sorin, CSC. Or the legendary football coach and marketing visionary, Knute Rockne. Maybe it's renowned leader, civil rights luminary, and president who rocketed Notre Dame to academic and international fame, Fr. Ted Hesburgh, CSC. Or the beloved professor, theologian, and trail-blazing rector who inspired generations of women and men, Sr. Jean Lentz, OSF.

If you're like me, you might not immediately think that a native Hawaiian, faithful Mormon, and former linebacker whose life was turned upside down by the media would be the ideal figure to represent a Catholic university in northern Indiana. But I would add the name Manti Te'o to any list of people who I think best represent the ideals and virtues we wish to instill in all who graduate from Notre Dame.

Manti graduated from Notre Dame in 2012 with a list of accolades and awards that seems impossible for one person: the Maxwell Award, the Walter Camp Player of the Year

Award, the Lott IMPACT Trophy, the Chuck Bednarik Award, the Bronko Nagurski Trophy, the Butkus Award, the Lombardi Award—and he was unanimously named an All-American. I and many others think he was robbed of the Heisman because of the media circus surrounding his personal life that would have left nearly anyone scarred and resentful for decades.

Not Manti.

I met him on the sidelines soon after a 2022 documentary about him was released on Netflix, *Untold: The Girlfriend Who Didn't Exist*. It's a fascinating and heartbreaking story that left me with an overall sense of incredulousness. It wasn't that I couldn't believe this had happened—rather, the thing that most surprised me was Manti's ability to forgive and rise above it all. We chatted a bit when I first met him in the north end-zone of Notre Dame stadium on September 17, 2022, when Notre Dame played Cal. I told him that I had recently watched the documentary and thanked him for being an inspirational witness to the power of forgiveness. He was humble, grateful, and quickly turned the conversation to thank me for what I'm doing with the team. More than ten years later, he was still acting like the legendary captain he was.

At the beginning of the 2024 season, Manti came to speak to the whole team. I wasn't at the team meeting when he spoke, but I have watched the video of it many, many times. He said, "There's a quote that I always live my life by. And that's a quote by Winston Churchill, and he said, 'History will be kind to me because I intend to write its pages.'"

Scan the QR code or visit www.tinyurl.com/manti-teo to watch Manti Te'o address the team before the 2024 season.

He continued, looking around at the team, gathered in the auditorium, "If you're in this room, you have one thing that millions of people outside don't have. And that's this." He held a pen in his right hand and paused.

"It's the ability to write history. *You* have that. I was able to write a lot of things when I was here, a lot of records when I was here. But there's one thing that I wasn't able to write—we got close—that was a national championship."

He turned to Coach Freeman and said, "Coach," as he walked over to him and handed him the pen. "You ready."

He looked at the players and said confidently, "You boys ready."

That insight and that pen became a powerful symbol for the 2024 season. Before and after several of our games, Coach Freeman held it up and reminded the team that they had the ability to write history. As the season progressed, this took on more and more meaning for the team as they bounced back from a stunning and seemingly impossible loss to Northern Illinois at the home opener of the season. Game after game, the Irish found a way to win. They fought off a comeback from Louisville, rolled over a talented Florida State team, beat an undefeated Army team at Yankee Stadium, and had two epic pick-sixes (interceptions returned for a touchdown) against Southern Cal to finish the regular season 11–1. And then they beat Indiana in the first round of the playoffs. And then Georgia in the Sugar Bowl. Finally, they came out on top over Penn State in the Orange Bowl. It turned out that Manti was right: They were indeed ready. The Irish had made it to the National Championship game in Atlanta versus Ohio State.

Right before we took the field for that championship game, Coach Freeman gave an epic pregame speech as we all took a knee. At the conclusion, he knelt, too, and we all joined hands

to pray the Our Father as we did every game. Then comes my part: "Our Lady, Queen of Victory!" And the whole team shouts in reply, "PRAY FOR US!"

Usually that's the moment I step to the side to avoid a stampeding team of very large and very psyched young men who are all ready to run through a wall. But Coach Freeman turned to me and put his hand out.

"Fr. Nate." He handed Manti's pen to me. "Hold on to this."

I think I just took it from him and nodded, but in my mind, this moment happened in slow motion, as though I was Frodo being handed the One Ring, Harry Potter grasping the Elder Wand, or Luke Skywalker receiving his father's lightsaber from Obi-Wan Kenobi.

Then my nerdy ruminations were interrupted by a second thought that made my stomach sink in anxiety and dread: *Don't lose it!* I jammed it in my pocket as we left the locker room, still reeling from being entrusted with this pen. *THE* pen. When we got to the sidelines, I took it out of my pocket and looked at it. It was just a normal pen. Just a plain, blue, retractable pen like one you would find in any office supply store.

But of course, this was more than a pen—it was a symbol. From its beginning, the Christian life has been filled with symbols. Jesus loved to use images and symbols in his masterful stories to teach about the kingdom of God and the truths of our faith. He talked about sowers, seeds, sons, and salt to illuminate his points. He invoked vines and branches, a prodigal son, and a good Samaritan so that people could understand and remember his teaching. Almost always, he used something tangible and imbued it with meaning—he used visible and ordinary things to communicate invisible, extraordinary realities to us.

Manti could have made his point using only his impassioned voice, but he handed Coach a pen. From that moment on, it was no longer an ordinary pen—it carried new meaning. Every time our student-athletes saw it, they were taken back to Manti's encouragement that if they seized this moment and gave their all, history would be kind to them as they sought to write its pages.

The National Championship game didn't go as we hoped, although I truly believe our team played their hearts out and should be nothing but proud of the way that they showed their character in the face of adversity. At the end of Manti's speech at the start of the season, he concluded by saying this goose-bump-inducing line: "I love you boys. I'm not gonna wish you luck, 'cause luck is for those that don't belong." Although we didn't win the national championship that year, we certainly proved that we belonged in that game. I'm immensely proud of our entire season.

In the locker room after the title game, there was no good moment to give Coach his pen back. He was consoling and encouraging our guys, telling them to keep their heads up and be proud of what they had accomplished. Then he was spirited away to talk to the press. On the bus back to the hotel, the pen almost fell out of my pocket twice, and the next day I was determined to give it back to Coach before it happened a third time. During the flight home, I thought about what I might say to Coach—was this a moment of sympathy or encouragement? How could I communicate to him how proud I was to be associated with this team and how grateful I was for this truly incredibly season?

When we arrived back at Notre Dame's campus, I walked up the stairs of the Gug to the second floor where his office is located. Coach Freeman was talking to Ron Powlus, and I knocked on the open door. I took a couple steps inside his office and decided that I didn't need to say much of anything in that moment. I just handed the pen to him and said, "Still a lot of ink left." He and Ron smiled, and as I walked out, he said, "Appreciate you, Fr. Nate."

I turned my head and smiled too. "Appreciate you, too, Coach."

\\\\\\\\\\

PRAY LIKE A CHAMPION

Today, pray for Our Lady's University, Notre Dame, that the men and women who live and work there might be faithful to God's call to be a force for good in the world. Our Lady of Victory, pray for us!

\\\\\\\\\\

FOOTBALL

ACKNOWLEDGMENTS

Writing this book has been a journey of faith, joy, and gratitude. It would not have been possible without the unwavering support of so many incredible people.

First and foremost, I extend my deepest gratitude to the student-athletes, coaches, and staff of the Notre Dame football team. You are the heart and soul of this story, and your indomitable spirit, true dedication, and deep faith have shown me the face of Jesus time and time again.

I want to thank Coach Marcus Freeman for writing the foreword to this book and for creating a culture of support for the spiritual well-being of our staff and team. Your leadership, care for others, and deep faith inspire me and so many others.

Also, a huge word of thanks to members of Notre Dame Athletics who were instrumental in helping me get permissions and assemble all of the pieces for this book, especially Katy Lonergan, Claire Cunningham, and Hunter Bivin. I really appreciate your commitment to excellence in everything you do.

To Fr. Mark Thesing, CSC, my predecessor as chaplain to the team: Thank you for believing in me and passing along so much wisdom in the kindest way possible. Your tip, "Eat every *time* they feed you, but don't eat every *thing* they feed you," was about the sagest advice I could have received! Your texts after every game mean so much to me.

I want to thank Coach Brian Kelly for your hospitable welcome as I started out as chaplain and for hiring an amazing staff. Finding my place on the team those first couple years was a challenge, and I am deeply thankful to Dr. Jerry Hofferth, Dr. Brian Ratigan, Dr. Chris Balint, Rob Hunt, Hunter

Bivin, Olivia Mitchell, Ron Powlus, Jason Michelson, George Heeter, and Jerome Keultjes for your warm welcome and support in those early years. Your countless acts of kindness made me feel a part of the Notre Dame football family.

I am profoundly grateful for the invaluable feedback and encouragement provided throughout the process of writing this book by my dear friend Bishop Bob Lynch. You have taught me so much about good storytelling, generosity, and the compassion of Jesus that you live out on a daily basis.

To my unofficial life coach, Amy Seamon; my bourbon and biking buddies Tim and Trish Maher; and my dear yoga coffee pal Stacey Noem. Your emotional support is a lifeline to me and kept me going through the many times I wasn't sure if I would make it across the finish line with this project.

To my loving parents, Dan and Sue Wills, my first models of faith and the unconditional love of God. From cookies to Christmas lights, you taught me to look at the world with wonder, excitement, and joy. I'm forever grateful for your love and countless sacrifices, Mom and Dad.

To my wonderful siblings, Nick and Natalie, and their beautiful families, Anita, Sam, Jack, Joe, Jimmy, Annemarie, and Mack: Thank you for your constant love and support. Nick, your presence throughout this book is a testament to the way I have always looked up to you with love and admiration. Natalie, you were not featured in this book (despite your constant questions as to what nice things I might say about you), but you feature prominently in my heart! You are always ready to celebrate my wins and ever present when I'm feeling defeated.

To my fellow Holy Cross priests and friends, Fr. Pete McCormick, Fr. Gerry Olinger, Fr. Greg Haake, Fr. Stephen Koeth, Fr. Dave Halm, Fr. Dan Parrish, Fr. Jim Gallagher, and Fr. John DeRiso: Thank you for your deep brotherhood in Holy Cross and your patience as you listened to all of these stories as they unfolded. You help me keep our shared mission and journey toward Jesus through his priesthood at the center of my life. Thanks to Fr. Bob Dowd, CSC; Fr. John Jenkins, CSC; and our provincial administration; who allow me to do this ministry with our team. I'm grateful for your leadership and support!

I want to thank Mary Ann and Jack Remick, Mark and Karen Rauenhorst, Joe and Jo Ann White, the whole Hyer family, Ron and Deborah Krantz, Mark Baumgartner, the Kalscheurs, and the Burkes for your support, fellowship, and prayers over the past several years.

To my dear friends Sean McGraw and Kris Trustey: Thank you for never missing a chance to build me up, help me find confidence in my voice, enjoy every mile, and share life in family and friendship.

A huge word of thanks to all of my colleagues and students in the Remick Leadership Program within the Alliance for Catholic Education (ACE) and the Institute for Educational Initiatives. Your witness and work in Catholic education help me see Jesus in the world on a daily basis.

A special and heartfelt thank you to my dear friend and mentor Fr. Mike Burke, who passed away in 2020. Your wisdom and example, cultivated over more than forty years as chaplain for the Wisconsin Badgers, laid the foundation for my own ministry when I was in grad school. Your family, parish, and friends (especially Judy, Hans, Kenny, Jeff, John, Ringer, and our dearly departed Jimmy) have found a deep place in my heart, and I will forever be grateful for the countless ways you shaped my life. You'd be proud, my friend: We're keeping hope alive.

Thank you to the great design and marketing teams at Ave Maria Press and my copyeditor, Patrick McGraw. You all were so fun to work with throughout this journey.

Finally, to my great friend and editor, Josh Noem: Thank you for your tireless work, guidance, and unwavering belief in this project. Your expertise and dedication made this book a reality, and your encouragement helped make every step of this project a joy.

Thank you to all who have read this book and have passed it on to others! God bless you, and Go Irish!

84
50

Fr. Nate Wills, CSC, is the chaplain of the University of Notre Dame football team. As an education professor at Notre Dame, he teaches in the Mary Ann Remick Leadership Program and is the founding director of the Alliance for Catholic Education's Higher-Powered Learning program, which helps teachers and leaders leverage technology to meet the needs of all learners in K–12 classrooms.

Fr. Nate earned master of divinity in theology and master of education degrees from the University of Notre Dame, as well as a doctorate in education leadership and policy from the University of Wisconsin–Madison.

Fr. Nate was ordained in the spring of 2006 and served as the associate pastor at Saint Joseph Parish in South Bend, Indiana, from 2006 to 2009.

He speaks around the country to teachers and administrators on artificial intelligence in Catholic education, blended learning, innovative uses of technology, and leadership in Catholic schools.

Instagram: @praylikeachampiontoday
YouTube: @praylikeachampiontoday

Founded in 1865, Ave Maria Press, a ministry of the Congregation of Holy Cross, is a Catholic publishing company that serves the spiritual and formative needs of the Church and its schools, institutions, and ministers; Christian individuals and families; and others seeking spiritual nourishment.